KIDS,
CRIME
& CHAOS

KIDS, CRIME & CHAOS

A World Report on
Juvenile Delinquency

ROUL TUNLEY

HARPER & BROTHERS, PUBLISHERS, NEW YORK

TO CARL W. HAMILTON

without whose help the author
might have become a juvenile delinquent

CONTENTS

ACKNOWLEDGMENT

IN 1958, the W. M. Armistead Foundation, supported by contributions from N. W. Ayer & Son, Inc., made a grant of $100,000 to the Greater Philadelphia Movement for the purpose of bringing together significant information on juvenile delinquency and preparing a study with specific conclusions that might be useful in helping communities control the problem. As a result, GPM turned to the University of Pennsylvania, a committee was formed, and Dr. James Bossard, of the University, was appointed to undertake the project. After eight months of work, which were ended by his death, I was appointed to complete the study. I would like to express my appreciation to Dr. Bossard for his efforts in getting the work under way and to the University of Pennsylvania, under whose general aegis the work was carried on. I would also like to thank the following members of the GPM's juvenile delinquency committee for their understanding in permitting me to turn a national survey into an international one and in letting me study our American problem in such unlikely places as Moscow, Bangkok, Tokyo, Tel Aviv, Cairo and other foreign cities in an effort to discover common denominators for a world-wide dilemma:

Howard C. Petersen, chairman
Walter E. Alessandroni

Harry A. Batten
Joseph F. Burke
Clifford Frishmuth
William F. Kelly
John Miner
Richard J. McConnell
I. M. Scott
Dr. Leslie R. Severinghaus

I am especially grateful to William H. Wilcox, executive director of the Movement, for his day-to-day encouragement and assistance.

FOREWORD

HOW THE BOOK CAME TO BE

WRITTEN

"WE need another book on juvenile delinquency like a hole in the head!"

This was the greeting hurled at me when I went to interview a Philadelphia commissioner in preparation for this book. It was not the first such comment I'd received, nor—as things turned out—the last. And although this sort of thing might discourage some people, it didn't discourage me. In fact, I agreed with it. The commissioner, I knew, is typical of many people working in the field. For more than a decade now, books on juvenile delinquency have been ground out of the presses like sausages—and are just about as digestible. Why, then, another "sausage"?

My reason is snobbery—in reverse. Most books on the subject—in fact, just about all of them—are written by experts. I am not.

The idea of a book by a nonexpert—a layman—is more or less novel. But why not? I asked myself. In the last analysis, it's the layman who produces, nourishes and pays the final bill for the delinquent product. He is called upon to finance, with taxes or private contributions, the various measures which the experts, acting through the politicians, create to prevent, control or, as often happens, proliferate delinquency. Many people believe that the public has made a mistake in abdicating in favor of the experts. They believe the time

has come for the public to take a look over the expert's shoulder and
see what they are getting for their money.

This arbitrary notion received direct impetus about a year and a
half ago when a group of public-spirited Philadelphians, who call
themselves the Greater Philadelphia Movement, came to me and
asked me to make a study of juvenile delinquency. Since I felt like
the commissioner whose comment opens this book, I turned the
project down. Furthermore, I pleaded lack of professional knowledge. Of course, I was a reporter but this did not qualify me as an
authority in a highly complex field. Why not give the job, I urged, to
some sociologist, psychiatrist or social worker, some scientist in the
field?

The GPM, I learned, had already done just that. A few months
before, they had entrusted the work to a highly competent professional, the University of Pennsylvania sociologist, Dr. James Bossard.
Unfortunately, Dr. Bossard died shortly after the project got under
way. After a few months of soul-searching, the GPM came to me.

To my negative response, the gentlemen of the GPM turned a
deaf ear. I don't know exactly why they persisted, and perhaps now
that they have their report—which also happens to be this book—
they will shake their heads and realize they should have taken "No"
in the first place. But the fact is that they *did* persist. They argued
that a nonprofessional was exactly the sort of man they now wanted.
They had made some inquiries and found that most books on the
subject were indeed written by professionals *for other professionals.*
Perhaps, they argued, a book by a member of the public, someone
who was not wedded to any theory or approach, was just what was
needed.

Their argument made sense. Besides, as the reader of the next
chapter will see, my travels as a reporter had already raised a few
questions which the experts seemed unable to answer. Without
further delay, therefore, I embarked on the journey that led to this
book.

Once under way, I couldn't have had more understanding bosses.
They agreed with me that, although Dr. Bossard's sociological approach had been a valid one, it might be a mistake for me to try to
graft it onto my own approach. They gave me a free hand to start

afresh and pursue my inquiries in my own reportorial way. They even went along, with only a few raised eyebrows (and the eyebrows of the GPM are awesome indeed), with the revolutionary notion that I could understand Philadelphia's, and America's, juvenile problems better if I abandoned these shores entirely for a while and took a trip around the world to do what no other person had yet done: examine our own problems in the light of what other people were doing about theirs.

Best of all, they never tried to press on me their own opinions, a truly remarkable feat inasmuch as I soon learned there is no subject on which people have such definite, violent and often misguided opinions. Although they footed the bills for my journey not only around the globe but up, down and across America, they never once suggested a panacea.

I am not so reticent, of course, and I now offer mine. If some of the members of the GPM are a bit startled to see the conclusions of this odyssey through the troubled waters of youthful misbehavior, I will not be surprised. A few may shrug their shoulders and arrive at a decision I reached early in my travels: namely, that more nonsense is spoken and done in the name of combating juvenile delinquency, and more confidence men and panacea peddlers are allowed to flourish in the field, than in any other legal occupation.

I don't expect that all readers will agree with what I found. Most certainly, few of the professionals will. But, not long ago, Americans in a national poll said that, apart from the issue of peace and national survival, they were more interested in juvenile delinquency than in any other problem. This, then, is primarily for them. It sums up an enlightening year and a half of looking, asking and digging by someone with no ax to grind, no vested interests to protect and no special equipment save a reporter's ball pen and a few refills.

PART I

THE DISEASE

"I WISH WE HAD SOME

DELINQUENCY . . ."

ALTHOUGH this book began officially in 1960, it really began unconsciously several years before when I was en route to a holiday in Sicily. I was talking to the mayor of a small town in southern Italy.

"I wish we had some of that juvenile delinquency you have," he said. "We could use it." He spoke with a wistful, faraway look in his eye, as though this desirable goal were unattainable.

"You mean delinquency's a good thing?" I asked in astonishment.

"Well, I wouldn't say it's exactly a *good thing*," he hedged. "But we could use the good things that always go with it—those nice, new factories, the new houses, the motorcars. In short, prosperity!"

Like most Americans, I was already confused on the subject. This confused me even more. The idea that prosperity was responsible for our delinquency when I had been told for years that it was poverty and slums and depressed living conditions was more than I could accept. I must have looked bewildered.

"You don't believe me," he said, squinting at me with shrewd eyes. "But look at it the way I see it. Down south here, we have no money, no industry, no progress. Nobody goes anyplace because they can't afford it. Besides there are no cars. The family is close; the church is strong. We have crime, of course—vendettas and bandits

3

and robberies—but that's a serious business, far too serious to trust
to children. We leave it to the grownups. Consequently, we have little
delinquency. Now, up north things are different. Everything's hum-
ming. New factories are going up, people are moving to the cities,
there's full employment, and everybody's buying automobiles and
apartments. The result? They've got delinquents all over the place!"
He made a wide gesture, very Calabrian.

I nodded but said nothing. After a while, he continued. "Look at
your own country. You had a low rate of delinquency in the years of
the Depression. Now things are better and you've got a lot more.
You're just paying the price of prosperity."

I'll call the mayor "Signore Canali" because he knew I was a
journalist and he asked me not to use his name. He was, after all, a
successful politician, and successful politicians don't go around saying, in effect, that juvenile delinquency is a sign of people on the
march, a badge of honor to be worn high on the sleeve. What would
his constituents think?

At that time, of course, I had no reason to use his name. I was not
on a story. We had simply been introduced by friends while I was
on a vacation. I had nothing to do for ten days but drive to Taormina,
perch myself on that towering pinnacle, and listen to the waves of
the sea seven hundred feet below.

Of course, it didn't turn out quite that way. The waves, except for
the cries of a few spoiled, middle-aged delinquents which floated up
to me, had a way of echoing back Signore Canali's words. They
tugged at my curiosity.

Although juvenile delinquency was not my specialty, I'd done a
few articles on various aspects of it and, like most Americans, I
found it baffling. Even more baffling were the official explanations.
And now that a thoughtful Italian had presented a fresh slant on the
subject, it seemed to raise all sorts of questions that had been lurk-
ing in corners of my mind, questions that had not taken form until
now.

I wondered, for example, why, if juvenile delinquency is primarily
a lower-class, underprivileged, slum-and-poverty condition, as our
sociologists and social workers had been telling us, progressive Swe-

den, which has abolished both poverty and slums, had the fastest-growing delinquency in the world.

I wondered why the West Germans, with their glittering new economy, their shiny Mercedes-Benzes and their bustling industries, had a soaring delinquency rate while the newly arrived East Germans in their midst—depressed, threadbare and under-privileged—behaved in a manner comparatively faultless.

I wondered why Japan, growing economically at a fantastically rapid rate of progress, had the worst delinquency problem in the Orient while Hong Kong, bursting at the seams with refugees and poverty, had none. I wondered why backward, illiterate Turkey boasted it had no juvenile delinquency, while Israel, vigorous and pushing, admitted its rate had doubled in a decade.

Did any of these things offer a clue to our own problem?

When I was back in the United States writing articles, intriguing bits of information came floating in from other countries from time to time—things that seemed to nibble away at the orthodoxy of our experts' thinking and to challenge our fondest shibboleths. A few favorite conclusions from recent delinquency conferences at home stood out in sharp contrast to the facts from abroad:

1. "Too many American women are working outside the home. That's the biggest factor in the rise in delinquency."

And yet a report from Austria, where the delinquency rate is low, showed that Vienna had the highest rate of working mothers in the world—50 percent.

2. "We need more and better psychiatric help for our delinquents, who are primarily sick children."

But here again, Austria, which invented psychoanalysis, used little psychiatry in its approach to the problem, relying on more inexpensive, down-to-earth techniques.

3. "We must have more money for more services."

But are we using what we have to the best advantage? Millions of dollars go into the same large, ineffective institutions year after year without a thought to developments in other countries, developments, for example, like the "halfway house," which is now considered a necessity in most places. Desperately poor countries like Egypt and

India wouldn't dream of letting a child who has been imprisoned return to his former life without first spending a certain amount of time in one of these homes, a kind of decompression chamber which gradually prepares him for the pressures of normal life.

4. "We need more daring and imaginative approaches to the problem of delinquency."

This is a favorite cliché at conferences, and yet few people in charge are daring enough to adopt some of the most successful innovations already operating right in our midst. Boston's deceptively simple Citizenship Training Program, which has reduced recidivism (return to crime) on the part of children who come before the courts to an astonishingly low 23 percent, has been all but shunned in the rest of the country although it's been operating for more than a quarter of a century. On the other hand, England has copied the program with excellent success.

Moreover, Highfields, the unorthodox New Jersey treatment center, which has chalked up a decade in treating young first offenders for about one-third the cost of conventional institutions, has been largely ignored by our own experts while Scandinavia and other countries get ready to adopt its features.

But most of all, the information that disturbed me was that in some countries juvenile delinquency was going *down*. Why? When I asked the question here, nobody seemed to have the answer. Furthermore, nobody seemed particularly inclined to look beyond the borders of his own parish for that answer.

This seemed strange because on most subjects Americans are constantly comparing themselves with others, both here and abroad. Our big industries are constantly exploring what's being produced in the rest of the world. Our doctors, lawyers, educators, chiropractors and plumbers are constantly attending international meetings and rubbing shoulders with their opposite numbers. Our government studies other governments and other peoples endlessly. But our delinquency experts are strictly stay-at-homes. And their thinking reflects it.

We have, of course, attended a United Nations conference or two on the subject. Several experts have been sent abroad by the Ford Foundation to study the penal systems of a few countries, and an inquisitive San Francisco judge, Mary Kohler, took a look at delinquency in five European nations and wrote a provocative article about it in the *Saturday Evening Post*. But until I began this study, I found nothing had been written on juvenile delinquency "in the round." In effect, we have remained smug, even indifferent.

Consequently, as I started to wend my way through the dense thicket of theories, doctrines and "true beliefs" in this country—such things as the effect of working mothers, boys clubs, psychiatry, gang infiltration, community action, clinics, Big Brothers, parent education, schools and the rest—I began to wonder how many Signore Canalis there were in the world to upset the apple carts of our own ideas in dealing with kids, crime and chaos. In no time at all, I came to a larger question, one which had been haunting me, unasked, for many months: Have the experts failed?

2

HAVE THE EXPERTS FAILED?

NOT long ago, in a brilliant article in *Harper's* on social workers, Marion K. Sanders said that if we were involved in an all-out nuclear attack tomorrow, the next day the doctor would be out treating burns, the minister would be running soup kitchens, the policeman would be herding children into rubble heaps where the teacher would be holding improvised classes. But the social worker, she said, would be busy holding a conference on "Interpersonal Relationships in a Time of Intensified Anxiety States."

To a layman like myself, suddenly entering the strangely impersonal, academically aloof, and status-conscious world of the experts, this parody hit home. "Nobody *ever* sees any children," an acid-tongued sociologist advised me when I was doing a round of interviews among child experts at a Western university. "They just see their slide rules."

What seemed even more curious was that these professionals in the field rarely see each other, especially if they represent divergent schools of thought in approaching the problem. Consider, for example, what happened to another layman, playwright Arthur Miller, when he crossed over into the world of the experts.

Feeling he might like to write a film play about juvenile delinquency, Mr. Miller invited to his home a group of fourteen experts

—men and women who had been recommended as serious students of the problem. But when they got together and started talking, he was more confused than before. Describing what happened in an article in *Book Review,* he wrote:

> One [expert] saw it from the psychiatric viewpoint, another from the statistical viewpoint, another from the settlement house viewpoint, and so on. Several things surprised me about this meeting . . . but the main thing was that this was obviously the first time they had ever met one another. Each one had his set of undeniable facts, and yet by the end of the evening, I had again to ask myself, as I said farewell to them—what causes delinquency? . . .
>
> The psychiatrist, despite his adeptness at treating disturbed kids, had to concede that at the rate he was going we would need thousands of psychiatrists in New York City alone. And what happens when the youngsters go back to the environments that disturbed them in the first place? The settlement house leader had the means to take kids in off the street for a few hours a day, and the statistician could predict with high accuracy which children in a particular school would turn to delinquency. *But no one of these disciplines could cure delinquency.*

Mr. Miller was experiencing the bewilderment of almost everybody who enters the special world of those professionals who deal with juvenile delinquency. Because of their insistence on their own method of handling the problem and their impatience with any deviation from this orthodoxy, one is apt to end up feeling he has been moving in a nihilistic jungle. And perhaps the biggest factor producing the dense undergrowth is the language. Although at one time or another I studied Latin, Greek, German, French and Italian at school —and even taught English at a university—I found these assets of little use in picking my way through the thick jargon of those chosen to deal with our delinquent children. It may not be typical but one of the first samples of this kind of talk which caught me up short was a psychiatrist's speech. He was describing his experiences working in a boys' training school to a group of people interested in the school's welfare.

"Unseen and unheard," he said, "but always omniscient are the subtle and covert resistances inevitably encountered when a con-

trapuntal modality invades the province of a re-educational discipline
which has long adhered to the conviction that behavior patterns can
be incrusted on a child by imprecation and admonition.''

In another lucid passage, he suggested: "The adjudication of a
delinquent as such imposes secondary and psychological layers which
further cement his alloplastic responses of aggression and hostility."
If he wasn't having much luck with his charges, I suggest that they
couldn't tell what he was talking about.

Not all juvenile delinquency experts are so hard to understand, of
course, but there is an increasing tendency for them to retreat into a
special caste talk which sets them apart—like ancient Egyptian priests.
Talk to a sociologist who has the full complement of university
degrees—and no profession is so avid of degrees—and the air becomes torpid with status words, known only to the initiate. Finding
a job for a kid is never just that, for example; it's "environmental
manipulation." And according to the previously quoted Miss Sanders,
social workers never just work in a school, a hospital or a welfare
office. They "function in a medical, educational or welfare setting."
Small wonder, as she says, that a twelve-year-old delinquent, exposed
to the lingo of the professionals during a stay in an institution, told
a reporter when he was released: "I've had two years of congregate
living, I've worked out my sibling rivalries, and I'm going home!"

This is not to say, of course, that the profession does not contain
fine, dedicated workers who love children and are trying to make
this a better world for them to live in. Nor is it to say either that
there are not strong critics of the profession *within* the profession,
those who deplore the double talk and the obscurantism and the lack
of realism. With becoming frankness, Dr. Eleanor Boll, a sociologist at the University of Pennsylvania, who has made a lifelong study
of family relations, declares: "I have found the general public a good
deal clearer and more intelligent than the experts in the field."

But in spite of such criticism from within, the fact remains that an
increasingly influential block of professionals has taken over a hu-
mane calling, separated it from the public by a curtain of recondite terminology, and attempted to turn it into a cool, exact science, much like
mathematics or nuclear physics. And because children simply won't
behave like microbes on a slide or atoms in a reactor, and because our

statistics tell us that delinquency is on the rise, the profession on the whole is as bewildered as the layman. No matter how turgid or obscure the vocabulary, nothing can hide that fact. Dr. Lloyd McCorkle, an expert himself and one of the country's outstanding criminologists, who pioneered as the director of Highfields, has said flatly, "The public is confused because the experts are confused!"

In an effort to determine just how much agreement exists among practitioners in the field, I made a cross-country tour of the United States, visiting most of the principal cities. I decided early in my travels to keep a record of the experts' responses. I asked all I interviewed three key questions:

1. *In your opinion, is delinquency on the rise?*
2. *Do you think it can be controlled?*
3. *If you had unlimited power to deal with the problem, what would you do first?*

I put my questions only to professionals in the United States since I did not feel this type of query would have much validity if extended overseas. And I put them only to leading figures—sociologists, psychiatrists, judges, reformatory superintendents, school authorities, gang specialists, etc.—working on the problem in all parts of the country.

Surprisingly, these brief questions often stopped them cold. The experts may have been working in the field for years, but they were so enmeshed in their own circles of activity that it was impossible for them to see the issue as a whole. One man, who has a towering professional reputation and has spent hundreds of thousands of the public's dollars doing research among city delinquents, said he simply had no idea what he'd do if he had the chance. "We need a social revolution," he finally said vaguely. When I pressed him further and asked him how he'd spend a million dollars if someone gave it to him to help control delinquency, he said, "Oh, that's easy. I'd just set up a study. After all, we don't really know what causes the problem."

In tabulating my questionnaire, preparatory to writing this book, I found that there was even more confusion among those handling the problem than I had anticipated. The only agreement at all was on the first two questions: i.e., the increase of delinquency and whether it could be controlled. A majority of those questioned (72 percent) felt that delinquency was either *not* on the rise or else they didn't know. Only 28 percent, a little over a quarter, believed what the public is told and what the statistics would seem to confirm: namely, that the rate of juvenile crime is going up. As might be expected, a whopping 94 percent agreed that delinquency could be controlled to a far better extent than it is now. Of course, since the problem itself forms the basis for their careers and livelihood, this kind of optimism was not surprising.

On the other hand, the third and crucial question—concerning what to do about it—revealed no agreement whatsoever. The majority could not get together on anything! (The experts, incidentally, were not limited in the number of suggestions they might make, and some made as many as half a dozen.)

The closest thing to a meeting of the minds—and it only amounted to 30 percent of the responses—was in two vague areas: (1) "More community support"; and (2) "Educate the parents."

The next most popular suggestion, which was mentioned by a quarter of those queried, was in the area of schools. They felt our delinquency-prevention potentialities were not being fully tapped in educational institutions. The next highest number endorsed "better police, court and probation work" (22 percent). And 17 percent just urged "more of everything," despite the fact, as we shall see later, that "more of everything" doesn't work. (This last suggestion, incidentally, was the conclusion of the latest White House Conference, a mammoth conclave of experts held in 1960.)

Curiously enough, at the bottom of the list were an equally interesting set of suggestions, *interesting because of the lack of enthusiasm they engendered.* A work program as an antidote for delinquency received the endorsement of only 6 percent of the experts. Religion evoked a similar lack of response. The emphasis on "morality and ethics" in the problem was even further down the list (less than 5 percent), while the control of mass media for children (television, movies, comic books, etc.) was about the same. Less than 5 percent, too, advocated what might be described as a "get tough" policy, despite the fact that such a point of view is frequently urged in local newspapers and undoubtedly is reflected in the attitudes of police and the courts.

All these responses are particularly interesting when compared with the attitudes of those dealing with children in foreign countries. Most of the experts overseas are diametrically opposed to our point of view. With far less money to spend on the problem and with a more exacting public breathing down their necks, they have been forced to adopt a more realistic, often imaginative approach, though not necessarily a "tougher" one. But we shall look at that later, since in this chapter we are concerned only with our home-grown experts.

In sum, there is less agreement and uniformity of approach—for better or worse—among the practitioners in this country than abroad. Why?

One obvious answer, of course, is that we are a bigger, more complex country, with more heterogeneity of problems. Another is that each avenue of approach has its special circle of devotees. Each group has an enormous stake—financially, ideologically and emotionally—in its chosen field and is interested in protecting this vested interest. The psychiatrist, as Mr. Miller has pointed out, is going to see the problem as one of inner conflict. The sociologist is going to view it as primarily one of "outer conflict," the result of environment. The biologist will see it as a physiological problem, and the FBI man will see it as a police one. The result is that each group tends to view the other group with suspicion, as a potential threat to his ideas, his livelihood, his lifework, or all three.

As might be expected, there are also groups within groups, as hostile to one another as outside groups. In Chicago not long ago I talked with a man who functions effectively as the leader of a group pushing better schools, probation, police and courts as an antidote for delinquency. This is roughly the "social" approach. When I mentioned the name of a man who was doing equally effective work as a leader of the "gang worker" approach—also "social"—he responded as though I were speaking of the leader of a hostile, even dangerous group. "That will never amount to a row of beans!" he shot back.

In Boston, I spoke unwarily to a famous sociologist about the admirable (and rare) simplicity with which Sheldon Glueck and his

wife had expounded their statistical approach to delinquency prevention in their celebrated books. My sociologist friend summed up his
reaction in few words. "They *think* simply, too!" he grunted.

This creeping anarchy, rampant in the realm of delinquency workers, is armed and supported by a fast-growing factor which tends to
slow up any all-out attack on our problem. This factor is our *pre-
occupation with research*.

The easiest way to tear down another man's carefully constructed
machine for combating delinquency is to announce: "But it hasn't
been proved!" This has led to a wild scramble to get on the growing
research bandwagon—oiled, greased and fueled by well-heeled and
well-meaning foundations.

Although 11 percent of those who responded to my questionnaire
listed "research" as a solution of the problem, most of them said in
discussion that before we embarked on any program we should "get
at the facts" by a program of "more and better research."

But just how effective is "more and better research"? Almost every
report urges it, almost every speech refers to it, and just about any
book ends up by calling for it.

Dr. Eleanor Boll, an old hand at conferences and other academic
séances on the subject, has declared that no matter what the experts said along the way, there were only two things that most of
them ended up asking for when the talks concluded: (1) more money
to hire bigger staffs "to do a better job"; and (2) more academic research.

Research, of course, is a basic necessity at some point along the
line. It helps people evaluate what they are doing. Up to a point it's
extremely worthwhile. In Europe it is generally conducted by people
outside the project being examined—lawyers, economists, statisticians
and others who might never get near the problem in this country.
Their recommendations are generally acted on promptly by the government, or by whoever is conducting the program. Some of the best
programs, however, like Austria's famous children's villages, have
never been evaluated. "Everybody just knows they're good," an
Austrian told me. "Just look at the children!"

In this country research staffs are sometimes set up as an integral
part of the program. The perpetrators of a project start out with a

hypothesis and build in a research group which *wants* the hypothesis to be proved.

In other cases, however, research in this country is conducted independently. Mostly, this is done in the universities by scholars who want either to prove one of their own theories or disprove someone else's. All one needs is a small—or large—grant, and away he goes, in a flutter of IBM cards.

The *New York Times Magazine,* in a recent article lamenting the fact that no one wants to teach any more, called research "one of the magic words in our vocabulary." It pointed out that in a recent tabulation of applicants for jobs as teachers in colleges and universities nine out of ten persons listed research as their chief or sole interest. In discussing the rewards for this kind of activity, the article concluded: "Often the more obscure the research, the farther the jump."

Not long ago, I talked to the head of a large research staff employed on a permanent basis by one of our Western states. His job is to evaluate juvenile delinquency treatment. The man had been working for three years but couldn't point to a single definite conclusion he or his staff had reached as a result of their efforts. In fact, my question, I felt, seemed naïve to him.

One of the troubles with research is that in theory it sounds fine but in practice it seldom seems to prove anything. If the reader of this book will try the following trick, he will see what I mean: The next time you meet someone working in the field of delinquency, ask him to point to a single—*just one*—fact that has been proved indisputably by research. My guess is that you will draw a negative response. I did, and so have others. Millions of dollars have been poured into research in the last ten years, and it's almost impossible to find an expert who feels that anything has been really proved. Sophia Robison, an authority on delinquency for New York City and the author of a recent hefty (532-page) book which examines and evaluates just about every delinquency program extant in the country, finally draws a blank (on page 529) on the value of research.

In speaking of the causes of delinquency she says: "*None* of the explanations . . . is satisfactory to any large group of people. Each of the attempted explanations of delinquency—in terms of individual characteristics, family types, community conditions, or culture conflicts—*has been inconclusive."* (The italics are mine.) In spite of this sobering conclusion, Miss Robison on the final page cheerfully urges "more and better research!"

One of the pitfalls of overconcentration on research, of course, is that it ends up being *an end in itself,* a kind of intellectual parlor game played by the academicians with a status-building degree as a door prize. At the very least, it proves the academicians are smarter than the next fellow. As a result, children—the reason for the research in the first place—seem to be less and less important. Perhaps this is why Dr. John Conrad, the criminologist who recently conducted a study of European penal systems for the Ford Foundation, told me: "The trouble with professionals in the United States is that they see delinquency as an intellectual problem with no particular concern for the people involved. What's more, if you want to work in the field and you just like people and want to help them, you probably won't get a job at all. You're suspect."

Many people who work on the firing line, dealing daily with kids who get in trouble, deplore the kind of "numbers game" which the academicians play in their ivory towers. "Very few people in the field seem actually to want to work with youngsters any more," said Jim O'Connell sadly. He is a young, attractive, Irishman with three kids of his own whom he has trouble supporting on the small salary he earns as a psychologist at the Fairfax, Virginia, Child Clinic. "They'd rather work with computers."

Another veteran of the firing line, Judge Mary Kohler, who is a mother herself, also finds the delinquency field "research happy."

"There is a great hesitancy in the United States today to say that something is good or bad unless it can be proved by statistics. Yet new forms of medicine have been adopted before there was substantive proof. I believe that God gave us wisdom before he gave us figures."

But if Mrs. Kohler is the first to admit that the experts, research-prone and degree-oriented, have failed to control our juvenile delinquency, she will admit with equal readiness that the real culprit may be the public. In her opinion, the average American has a blind faith in science to solve all our problems, even child behavior. And having abdicated in favor of the scientist, Americans keep pressing him for the answer, the magic formula.

"One of the reasons for all the mumbo jumbo," she says, "is that the experts are being pushed and they feel they must come up with something. The public may not be ready to believe the problem is as complicated as it is, and they may not be willing to pay the price of solving it when they have the answer."

Her point of view is echoed by many another student of the problem. Negley Teeters, the Temple University sociologist who teaches the only course in juvenile delinquency in Philadelphia, feels that our professionals take their cue directly from the public. "Americans insist on 'experts' for everything," he declares. "Even a janitor's got to be an expect; he's a sanitary engineer."

Certainly, a case for delinquency responsibility could be made out for either the public, the experts, or both. But at this juncture, the question, "Who's to blame?" seems beside the point. More to the point would be some general agreement on how to attack the problem in concrete terms. For the fact is that our present "scientific" approach, concocted by the experts and tolerated by the public, has produced little success. It has resulted in more chaos than clarity, and certainly very little agreement.

"The trouble with science, particularly research, is that it may *never* give us the answers," Dan G. Pursuit, an ex-probation officer and now one of the heads of the University of Southern California's Youth Studies Center, admitted in summing up the problem. "Children can't be reduced to an exact science. You can't develop a vaccine. People can't be captured in test tubes."

In view of the prevailing chaos among the ruling priesthood of delinquency experts, many laymen, and even enlightened professionals, are beginning to wonder if it isn't time for the public to get back into the act. Perhaps the "scientists" *are* lagging behind the average man.

One of the staunchest advocates of the need for the public to play a far greater role in our delinquency problems than they have been playing in the past is Dr. McCorkle, a curious combination of a scholar and a man of action (he was once warden of New Jersey's state prison).

"Let's take juvenile delinquency away from the experts," he insists. "They're committed to their own brand of magic. It's time to give it back to the amateurs—the parents, the teachers, the ministers, yes, even the politicians. After all, how scientific can you get!"

This may well be the answer. In any event, the public should be asking the experts some hard questions. But before they step in to do that, they have a right to know just how bad—or good—our juvenile delinquency is.

How Bad Is Our Delinquency?

Armed with the sturdy belief that our delinquents are the biggest, the best and the most delinquent in the world—something one gathers from reading our newspapers, watching TV and movie programs, and listening to the experts—I was in for something of a shock when I circled the globe.

In Sweden, I met Mrs. R., a pretty young American mother from Seattle who had two small daughters and was living in Stockholm because her husband had a job there. "As soon as my children reach their teens, I'm going to pack up and go home," she said decisively. "I wouldn't dream of letting my daughters grow up in this atmosphere!"

Sweden was one of the first countries I stopped in. The cool, placid beauty of Stockholm's lakes and the bustling air of efficiency and prosperity seemed an unlikely setting for youngsters to get into trouble.

"You have no idea what happens here," she insisted. "Just walk along the Kungsgatan any night and watch what goes on—wild teen-agers in hopped-up cars, drinking, sex, even dope." She paused and shook her head. "No, not for *my* girls. When the time comes, we're going home."

If this had been the lament of a Puerto Rican mother, living in

New York's Spanish Harlem, I could have understood more readily. But in lovely Stockholm where there are no slums, no poverty, no unemployment!

However, I wasn't in town long before two things happened which underlined Mrs. R.'s remarks. It was the fall of 1960, and during my short, ten-day stay, two juvenile murders took place, a high average for a city of only 700,000. One involved a nineteen-year-old boy who killed a ten-year-old boy in a sex crime, while the other concerned a seventeen-year-old who stabbed another boy his own age with a kitchen knife.

Furthermore, these were no isolated instances of violence. In 1957, a crowd of three thousand youngsters, most of them teen-agers, rioted against the police in Stockholm. They wrenched off car doors, overturned vehicles, frightened horses with firecrackers and bombarded the police with tin cans. Later, at Karlskoga, a town in western Sweden, five hundred boys and girls went wild at an auto race, raining bottles on the firemen who came to put out the fire in a building they'd put the torch to. Forty-five were eventually arrested, including a girl attired only in a brassière. At about the same time in Gallo, in northern Sweden, another riot by teen-agers armed with knives, air guns and bicycle chains resulted in the arrest of seventy boys and girls.

Checking into official figures, I was surprised to find that Sweden probably has the highest juvenile delinquency rate in the world, higher than ours. According to Karl-Erik Granath, director of the Child Welfare Council in Stockholm, *3 percent* of Sweden's teen-age youth go through their courts. This compares with *1.8 percent* in this country (or 2.3 percent if traffic violations are included). Furthermore, Sweden, with the second highest number of autos per capita of any country in the world (we are first), can boast of the highest percentage of car thefts by juveniles, thus putting our young auto-snatching hoodlums still further in the shade.

Turning from Sweden to Japan, the traveler finds conditions almost as astonishing. In this Oriental country, before World War II children were said to be among the most obedient and law-abiding of any nation on earth. Obviously, things have changed.

Even before looking into the statistics, the unwary visitor, fed on a poster diet of dainty Japanese girls in flowing kimonos moving along obediently behind their men, is apt to get a shock as he walks down the Ginza. Here, teen-agers, in skin-tight blue jeans and dyed red hair, cigarettes dangling from their lips, can be seen walking along with their arms around their boy friends. This unsettling picture, it turns out, is a suitable prelude to a look at the official figures. Although Japan's rate of delinquents brought before her courts is still lower than ours (1.2 percent), the *rate of climb* has far outstripped ours.

What's more, the ratio of crime committed by Japanese youngsters when compared with adults is out of all proportion to ours, showing juveniles acting far more lawlessly, compared with their elders, than ours do. For example, in Japan, teen-agers commit a whopping 21 percent of all the country's crime. Ours commit about 12 percent. Take one category—violent sex. In our own country, juveniles account for 19 percent of the total rapes. In Japan, they're in the majority—52 percent.

But perhaps the reader will still insist that we hold the edge in over-all violence?

Consider, then, the case of a seventeen-year-old Japanese who wandered into a ladies' rest room in a restaurant by mistake not long ago. When a woman attempted to admonish him for his behavior, he simply took out a knife and hacked her to death on the spot.

We tend to think we have a monopoly on misbehaving youngsters —a view encouraged by many foreigners envious of our material well-being. But such a "monopoly" does not square with the facts. The sweep of juvenile crime in certain places can match, or even top, our own brand. It is not true of all countries, of course, as we shall see. In some places, juvenile delinquency is under control, or even going down. But what interested me particularly was that in many countries abroad, even those with low rates, there was a new and alarming pattern of misbehavior. It indicated a purpose and organization which our own youngsters lacked. In fact, there were times when I wondered if our delinquents weren't a little backward.

Most of us remember, for example, that in the spring of 1960 a riot in Istanbul by a group of students, mostly in their teens, resulted in the fall of the Menderes government in Turkey.

At about the same time in Tokyo, the delinquent behavior of 76,000 students, rioting wildly outside the Diet building, forced President Eisenhower to cancel his visit to Japan. One may argue that such students were not strictly delinquents, but certainly similar behavior by teen-agers in front of our Capitol in Washington would have been labeled delinquent. In any event, not long after the riots, a seventeen-year-old boy, who had a two-year record of violence, stabbed and killed the Socialist party chairman, Inejiro Asanuma, and caused another upheaval in the government.

While our young students were doing such things as rolling beds, rocking streetcars, stealing girls' panties, or (at Harvard) demonstrating to keep their diplomas in Latin rather than English, their violent South Korean counterparts were toppling the long-standing government of President Rhee.

In still other countries, youngsters were committing acts of sabotage against the educational system—acts carefully organized with such objectives as changing the curriculum or removing administrators. Such things would have brought a hue and cry against "student hoodlums" in this country, and perhaps a movie, exported to the world, would have told all about it.

Gentle India, where the taxi drivers never shout at each other and where even the dogs seldom bark, has more evidence of this kind of dictatorship by the young than any other country. This is readily understandable. During the struggle for independence, children were often used by agitators in the various political parties to carry out demonstrations against the government. The result was that children learned all the tricks of civil disobedience. It was hard to unlearn these tricks when they had won independence but when they still had other goals to obtain—like getting independence from things they didn't like in school. Consequently, the student strike is a well-known phenomenon in India. While I was there, 3,600 students of the Pathumwan Technical Institute struck in protest against the transfer of their principal to a post in the Ministry of Education. Police were called out to handle the incident, and the Ministry promised to reconsider its decision.

Such things, in fact, are happening all over Asia. In Japan, during my visit to Kyoto, fifteen students were being tried for disrupting a lecture series at the university with the avowed purpose of getting the course changed. Even in Thailand, a country low in delinquency, the student riot against hard exams or a hard curriculum is a not-infrequent occurrence.

The fact is, of course, that juvenile misbehavior is a world-wide phenomenon, but the quality and the quantity vary widely from country to country. England has its "teddy boys," France its *"blousons noirs,"* Sweden its *"raggare,"* Germany its *"Halbstärken,"* and Japan its "thunder boys."

Even in Russia, where Communist doctrine proclaims that there is nothing in the nature of socialism that could give rise to crime, I found considerable evidence of juvenile delinquency—explained officially as "vestigial remnants of the old capitalist system."

"How can children who have never known capitalism commit crimes?" I asked.

"Well," the official said, "this is because such children are still under the influence of people who were born and raised in capitalist conditions." No country's experts ever had a better "out" for failure on their part to control the situation.

Although there is no official recognition of a delinquency problem in Russia and no published statistics, there is increasing reference to it in the press. Moscow's delinquents are called *stilyagi,* and incidents are mentioned only when the government wants to make a point. It may be against rock and roll music, buying foreign currency, espionage, wearing Western-style clothes, etc. But in making these points, the Soviets reveal the extent of their juvenile misbehavior, whether it be robbing telephone boxes, selling heroin, muggings, gang fights, beating up cops, drunkenness or just plain unwillingness to work.

From Moscow to Manila, and from Turin to Tokyo, delinquency as bad as or worse than ours does exist. And it may flourish in the most democratic or the most controlled of societies. But in many countries, as we shall see later, the problem is either diminishing or is definitely under control—such countries as France, Denmark, Belgium, Austria, most of Italy, and the majority of Oriental countries. Consequently at this point, and against this background of international behavior, it might be well to look at both the quality and the quantity of our own delinquency before taking up the factors that control the situation.

As the reader gathered from the questionnaire I used in the preceding chapter, there is considerable confusion in this country on just how delinquent our juveniles are. Among the experts queried, over half (56 percent) simply had no idea whether the rate was going down or up. This, of course, is in direct contrast to the situation which our government statisticians tell us exists.

Perhaps a word should be said here about statistics in general, especially those used in this book. As everybody in the field points out, the use of figures is a tricky business, and on this the experts are right. Methods of gathering, counting and comparing figures of juvenile delinquents vary from country to country and from state to state.

Consider one of our own towns—Jersey City, for example. In 1930, there were 1,974 youngsters brought to juvenile court. In 1954, a quarter of a century later, there were only 684. This represents a fantastic decline in view of the soaring national statistics. The casual observer, looking at these figures, might easily come to the conclusion that the sad, shabby little town of Jersey City might be the ideal place in which to bring up one's children. The facts behind the statistics, however, are these: In 1931, Mayor Hague, then dictator of the city, decided that it was a good idea to keep children out of juvenile court, whenever possible. He instituted a "police service bureau," an agency to drain off all possible cases, within the Board of Education. The results, as we have seen, sounded as though Jersey City had solved its delinquency problem, although this was far from the truth.

There are further factors complicating the statistics picture. In some states, a juvenile is no longer a juvenile after sixteen. In some, the figure is eighteen, and in foreign countries it is occasionally nineteen.

For these and other reasons, many experts refuse to make any comparisons at all. In order to be absolutely accurate, too many variances have to be explained. But for the layman, interested in over-all trends, this argument is weak. He is interested in general facts rather than in decimal-point accuracy.

If the reader will remember the possible pitfalls of statistics and that wherever possible the more obvious monkey wrenches in the machinery of numbers will be pointed out, I shall proceed to use figures in this book which will give the reader some broad idea of the situation at hand.

In this country there are only two agencies reporting juvenile delinquency nationally—the Children's Bureau of the Department of Health, Education, and Welfare and the Federal Bureau of Investigation. The former deals with children who are brought before the courts, while the latter includes those arrested by the police.

Although there are the usual complicating factors in making a comparison (the FBI, for example, counts only those under eighteen, while the Children's Bureau counts those of whatever age the state declares juveniles to be), the findings of the two agencies, gathered separately, parallel each other to a remarkable degree. *They both show strong upward trends.*

For simplicity, let's concentrate on the figures of the Children's Bureau, since both agencies paint the same picture, more or less. The Bureau, first of all, operates on a near-starvation basis. One man, I. Richard Perlman, the genial and hard-working head of the statistical branch, is, along with one assistant, the entire staff of the U.S. Government engaged in gathering national juvenile court statistics. His findings are based on samples, rather than complete figures, which are sent to him voluntarily. Some states don't report the numbers that reach their courts at all, and in such cases Mr. Perlman must make estimates. It is a makeshift arrangement for a great country, but there it is, nonetheless.

From where he sits, Mr. Perlman is convinced that delinquency is proliferating at a remarkable rate. Even discounting such reasons for a rise as better reporting, better police work, more interest on the part of juvenile crime agencies, and a "crack-down" attitude, he is confident that there is an upward trend, far outstripping the normal population rise.

In 1940, for example, 200,000 cases of delinquency were disposed of by the courts. This included those who violated traffic laws. In the middle fifties, however, it was decided not to include in the figures violators of traffic laws since the use of cars by juveniles had increased so markedly in the interim. Adjusted for this factor, the number of cases handled by the juvenile courts was estimated to be 514,000 in 1960. This better-than-150-percent jump occurred while the juvenile population as a whole was climbing only about 25 percent, and now accounts for almost 2 percent of our entire juvenile population.

As he sits in his office in Washington, D.C., and sees the figures of delinquency multiply year after year, it is small wonder that Mr. Perlman shakes his head skeptically and says, "In spite of all the explanations, I think there's been a *real* rise in delinquency. It's not just better reporting."

Why then do most of the people I talked to doubt the rise which the statistics seem to prove?

Part of the reasons are those we mentioned, reasons which can be put under the general heading of a greater awareness by people of the problem. There are more agencies to deal with delinquency, more stories by the press, radio and television, more police activity, more opportunity to uncover misbehavior that was left covered in other days.

Even more important, however, may be the growing touchiness of the public when it comes to delinquency—a rising impatience with deviant behavior. I am not talking about the tragic gang murders or the killings and rapes and robberies of innocent people by young hoodlums. These are deplorable and should be dealt with promptly and effectively without sentimentality.

But these are numerically as nothing compared with the vast majority of cases that swell the dossier of our statistics and terrify a public already alarmed about its youth. The truth is that we have broadened our definition of juvenile delinquency so recklessly in the last several decades that it includes just about every transgression of childhood. In fact, every reader of this book could easily have become a juvenile delinquency statistic at one time or another if present tension and present definitions had held sway in his day. In short, we are overjittery about our youngsters.

For example, in California, not long ago, three boys were arrested when they were caught swimming in a river without clothes. They became part of the "alarming" delinquency statistics Mr. Perlman refers to and which have convinced him the situation is worsening. And yet the fact is that a generation ago nude swimming in the old swimming hole was as much a part of the American picture as baseball or swiping Mom's cookies, and no one would have thought twice about it. On another occasion in the same state, another boy was detained for forty-eight hours in jail for jaywalking. Europeans find such things hard to believe.

These are extreme cases, of course, but they do dramatize a growing alarm which results in masses of youngsters being arrested for spitting on the sidewalk, violating curfew, running away, smoking and other relatively minor misdemeanors which used to be associated with the normal process of growing up. And once the label of delinquent is officially pinned on a youngster, it is hard for him to get rid of it.

Contrast our approach with that of other countries in this regard. In just about every other nation, a child is brought to court and tried *only if he breaks a law whose violation by an adult would also constitute a crime.* In this country, our definition of juvenile delinquency has been stretched to such an extent that children become part of our records if they commit any number of acts which would not be considered a crime if committed by an older person. Such things are truancy, stubbornness, leaving home, curfew violation, incorrigibility and other antisocial acts.

"The fact is that we're widening the net of what we call delinquency in a disturbing fashion," says I. J. Shain, assistant research chief for California's Department of Correction. "Some kids are held for days on minor charges. This amounts in effect to a sentence without a trial, and if done to an adult, would bring an outcry. In Los Angeles at the moment," he pointed out, "one thousand kids are now in detention; London, a city of eight million, never has more than a hundred at one time."

Mr. Shain also believes that increased services of police and institutions are good up to a point; after that, they merely promote the problem. With so many people looking for trouble and with their jobs, in fact, depending on finding it, many children, he believes, are picked up for offenses which might better be forgotten. "As soon as a new institution is built, it immediately becomes overcrowded," he says. "Judges feel it ought to be used." Pointing out that sixty thousand children are held each year in California detention homes, he said that many were there for crimes no more serious than walking across lawns, crossing streets against the lights, or being out after curfew.

A father himself, Mr. Shain is further disturbed by the fact that there is no agreement among officials in California as to the kind of treatment misbehaving youngsters should get. Far from being uniform or fair, it usually depends on the whim of geography. He points out that in San Diego County last year, 159 girls were reported for vagrancy. In adjoining Los Angeles County, enormously larger, with 40 percent of the state's entire population, in fact, only sixty-nine girls were so reported. Obviously there is far greater tolerance in the latter county toward vagrancy—a vague charge which can mean anything from walking along a street with no visible means of support to actually living with a man out of wedlock.

Another official who is unhappy not only about our method of compiling statistics but also about what he calls a "tendency to proliferate the problem through mass hysteria" is Milton Rector, director of the National Council on Crime and Delinquency.

"Many counties add juvenile police officers, and juvenile crime automatically increases," he said. "The press prints a lot of stories about delinquency, the heat is on, and the cop on the beat is more apt to book kids. I'm not convinced that juvenile delinquency is any worse than it ever was."

One of the interesting sidelights of the so-called American tendency to "promote delinquency by statute" was evident at a recent United Nations conference in London. The Americans found that in order to make any sort of valid comparison with the European representatives it was necessary to take out of our statistics those youngsters picked up for things a European would not be picked up for. The American delinquency rate automatically dropped 50 percent!

To an official abroad, this situation seems not only hard on the children, but shows a curious American determination to put one's worst foot forward—and to hell with the national image! It was something which amazed officials in other countries when I ran into them a few months after the London conference. In Switzerland, for example, which guards its image as jealously as the Lion of Lucerne, I talked with Dan Q. Moloch-Houwer, head of the International Union for

Child Welfare, about the subject. "You Americans like to throw all your dirty linen on the table," he said. "It's good to be frank, but you overdo it!"

In Egypt, Dr. Ahmad M. Khalifa, director of the Institute for Criminology and a one-time student in America, said, "You are over-estimating your delinquency because of your advanced methods of mass communication. It is not as bad as you think. Beware of overesti-mating the problem. You'll end by believing it and it'll be particularly hard on the kids."

In the opinion of some students of the problem, there may be still another reason for the sharp climb of the delinquency rate here other than the tendency of Americans to keep on broadening the base and making our definition vaguer and more all-encompassing. Negley Teeters, the Temple University sociologist, believes that the fact that most statistics start in the Depression or shortly thereafter—a period of low delinquency—makes our current figures seem startlingly high. Since almost no statistics have been reliably kept over a long period of time, it is impossible to get the long-range look at the problem that one might get, say, at the weather or the stock market, two other serious problems from time to time.

In a recent report to Congress on juvenile delinquency, it was stated: "There is some evidence that rates for juvenile delinquency also increased during the 1920's, when some features of our society resembled those of today, and declined again during the Depression years of the 1930's."

In this regard, it is interesting to look at some figures which Mr. Teeters, and his associate, David Matza, were able to dig up for as far back as 1918. They are for one specific locality—Cuyahoga County, Ohio—but they are interesting because they include one of America's larger metropolitan areas, the city of Cleveland.

In 1919, when World War I ended, the figures showed a delin-quency rate of children of 65.9 per 1,000. By 1920, the figure had dropped to 52, and by 1939, when the country was beginning to climb out of the Depression, the figure was down to 21. In 1957, however, the figure had swelled to 33.5. This represents an increase of 70 percent over the 1939 one, a period when our current statistics also began to soar. But compared with the post-World War I era, *they show an over-all drop.* Unfortunately, such figures do not exist for the country as a whole. If they did, we might easily find that all our comparisons are made with periods of low delinquency.

A few other factors may also help push up our present statistical peak. There are infinitely more automobiles around today than a generation ago—more autos to steal and to violate the laws with. There's also a more casual sale and use of guns, with much more money to buy them. Furthermore, there's a tendency to include more and more minors in the same charge. A newspaper story will state, "20 Youths Charged With Carrying Firearms" when only one of them actually possessed a gun. "Fifty-seven Youths Charged With Homicide," declared a headline recently, but it involved only one murderer. And as Mrs. Kohler pointed out in a recent article, a thousand youngsters were picked up and booked (and subsequently released) as a result of *one* gang killing in New York. All the youths, of course, became part of our national statistics.

But if official procedures may have changed over the years in picking up, counting and handling delinquents, many experts, including those who don't think the rate is up, are convinced that the problem has become more violent. In this, the public seems to concur.

This, however, is an all but impossible question to answer. Certainly, the zip guns, the switch blades, the lead pipes and the awesome arsenal of today's gang fighters would seem to be more lethal than the blackjacks, the knuckle dusters, the clubs and the other weapons which were used by the Irish and the Germans when their gangs terrorized the streets of New York City in the nineteenth century.

But as Anthony Sorrentino, the head of Chicago's Area Projects and an ex-gang worker himself, points out, fear, force, violence and destruction, always an integral part of American social life since the days of its earliest development, are more rampant today than yesterday. "In recent decades," he says, "we have engaged in two world wars, developed the atomic and the hydrogen bombs, nuclear weapons and other inventions which our citizens fear might destroy civilization and the human race. No wonder kids' weapons are more violent."

Testifying before a Senate subcommittee, Henry D. McKay, head of the Institute for Juvenile Research's sociological department, struck a similar note: "Perhaps the weapons used by young people are more lethal than those used several decades ago, just as the weapons used by nations are more deadly than those used in the past. But such changes do *not* establish an increase in juvenile crime."

One of the few studies undertaken to shed some light on the question of whether teen-age hoodlums are more aggressive today than in earlier times was undertaken recently by Jamesburg Reformatory in New Jersey. Studying the circumstances surrounding the commitment of boys eight to sixteen years old over the past thirty-five years, the investigators found that there had been no increase in the violence of the crimes. The only change over the years was one of color: more and more Negro boys were being admitted.

But whether juvenile delinquency is more violent or more widespread today than ever before should not obscure the fact that a serious problem does exist and that it can be controlled to a far greater extent than is being done at the present time. When all the figures and charts are weighed, discounted, corrected, adjusted and dissected, the fact remains that an extraordinarily large number of adolescent males are arrested, come before our courts and are labeled "juvenile delinquents." Although less than 3 percent of our juvenile population (including traffic violators) become annual statistics, the number takes on more importance when we consider the percentage of youngsters who will become court cases at least once *during their period of adolescence* (reckoned as an eight-year period). Looked at from this direction, it appears that 12 percent of our children are liable to become delinquents during their teens. An even more startling view may be obtained from looking at the boys alone, the real core of our problem. A recent study in Minnesota, for example, revealed that 22 percent of all boys in the ninth grade of the Minneapolis schools had appeared before the court, the police, or both within a period of two years. In the nation as a whole, if female delinquents are excluded from our statistics (and the proportion of girls to boys is one to eight), it will be shown that close to 20 percent of all our male adolescents get into trouble with the law and are hauled into court. This means that under our present setup *the American boy today has one chance in five of ending up in court as a juvenile offender.*

This sorry state of affairs is the result of both a hostile and unrealistic approach to the problem of childhood, as we shall see.

4

Do We Really Like Kids?

A few months ago, not far from my home in rural New Jersey, Fred, a tall, good-looking boy of fifteen, was picked up by the police at nine o'clock in the evening. He was looking at some pictures under a movie marquee. After a few minutes of questioning, he readily admitted that he'd run away from home and that he was hitchhiking. His family was living temporarily in England (his father was an Air Force major), and he was en route to a friend's home in Tucson, Arizona. He had just flown the Atlantic that day, having arrived at Idlewild only a few hours before. He had eight dollars in his pocket.

Fred was taken to Flemington, and lodged in a cell in the same jail where Bruno Hauptmann had stayed during the Lindbergh kidnaping trial. Charged with no crime, Fred was put in jail simply because there was no other place to put a runaway—a situation that prevails in *half the counties in the United States*.

Later, under questioning, Fred revealed that there was friction between his parents. He was unhappy. He'd tried unsuccessfully to leave home several times. This time he'd taken three blank checks from his mother's checkbook and signed her name to them, getting enough money to fly the Atlantic and get well on his way to Arizona. He had never been in trouble with the law before.

When his family was informed where Fred was, there was no hurrying to his side, no phone call to inquire about him. In fact, his father—a tall, handsome, crew-cut man of harsh visage—waited a full two weeks before flying to see the boy. Meanwhile, Fred remained in his barred cell. The warden, Harold Atkinson, and his wife, childless themselves, took a fancy to the boy and had him spend some time in their quarters. During this time, Mrs. Atkinson asked him one day if he'd like to live with them. "Would I!" exclaimed Fred with enthusiasm.

Finally, the father arrived at a nearby Air Force base. It was only three o'clock in the afternoon, but he made no immediate attempt to see his son. Instead, he spent the evening on his own. The next morning was Friday and he showed up at the court and promptly asked the judge, Joseph Halpern, if he couldn't leave his son in jail a few more days—over the weekend. He said he'd like to try to make arrangements for the son to stay with relatives in Virginia.

The astonished judge, whom Fred had struck as just about the ideal youngster to take anywhere, including Virginia, asked, "Why don't you take the kid with you?"

The father hesitated. Finally, he said lamely, "Because I'm afraid he might run away."

At this point, the judge became angry. The boy had already spent more than two weeks in jail although he'd committed no crime in this country. "I think you'd better take him with you," he said sharply. Reluctantly, the father agreed.

"I'm really going to catch it," murmured the boy to a reporter as the two prepared to leave. Judge Halpern hesitated for a moment and then stopped the boy. "If your father is not strong enough to help you, you help yourself, hear?" he said to the fifteen-year-old. The boy nodded gravely while the father stood by in silence. Then the two of them walked out of the courtroom, tight-lipped and walking apart, with little to link them together but the Jersey air.

Contrast this now with another father and son I ran across in Italy. The boy (I'll call him Guido) was approximately the same age, and he too had been picked up by the police. There had been a political argument (foreign youths seem to argue far more about politics than their United States counterparts), and Guido had wounded another boy in a pistol fight. The father found out about it shortly afterward when he came home from work. The first thing he did after inquiring about his son's health—even before he attempted to see him, hire a lawyer or go to the police—was to sit down and write his boy a letter. In it, he told Guido he knew little of the circumstances of the event but that he wanted the youngster to know that he had confidence in him and would stand by him no matter what had occurred. "Knowing you," he said, "I feel that whatever you did, I could easily have done the same under similar circumstances."

With the letter written and delivered, the father then went about the business of seeing officials, etc. Later, the boy, who spent five days in prison and was acquitted, told me that the most important thing that had happened to him in his whole life was receiving that letter with its assurance of his father's respect. It was obvious that in the future the boy would think twice before doing anything that might incur his father's displeasure.

You may say that these are two isolated and unusual cases, cited out of context, and that they could have happened in either country. You may be right. But I have chosen to cite them because they illustrate attitudes that I found typical of two different points of view regarding children: Abroad, people *expect* children to get into trouble and are delighted when they don't; in this country, they expect children to behave and are annoyed and frustrated when they don't. The result is that in America many people insist there exists what Judge Kohler has called a "climate of hostility toward children."

In discussing this attitude, Sophia Robison, in *Juvenile Delinquency*, declared that foreigners think us "hostile, impatient and rejecting of nonconforming youth." She feels that we "have too often forgotten our own adolescent rebellion and do not provide . . . controls without hostility. Instead . . . we give our youth the material advantages that our abundant resources make possible. And we are apt to be impatient when our children do not reward us with their good behavior."

In Italy, on the other hand, and in countries with low delinquency rates, I found an attitude toward children that was firm but at the same time warm and realistic. The whole community, in fact, seemed to line up in keeping a child reasonably happy and out of trouble. It was *everybody's* business, not just the parents! If a child misbehaved, the neighbor, with the complete approval of the parents, was apt to administer punishment on the spot.

Dr. Franco Ferracutti, Rome's distinguished criminologist, told me: "If a juvenile delinquent throws a stone at my car, I can get out and beat him up and get away with it. Even the kid's father would side with me."

In France, another country where delinquency is under control, I was astonished at the relaxed manner with which authorities viewed their teen-agers.

"What is a delinquent child?" Paul Lutz asked me rhetorically one day, when we were sitting in his office in the Place Vendôme. He is a deputy director of the French Ministry of Justice and one of the country's leading authorities on juveniles. "You and I were both delinquent at one time or another. Almost all children are. When I was eight, I started a fire in the clothes closet. Our house could have burned down and I would have been picked up as an arsonist. Luckily, neither thing happened."

Pointing out that runaways, truants and many other children who become officially delinquent in the United States would not be considered delinquent in France but are handled informally, Dr. Lutz said, "In France, we try to keep the label of delinquency away from a child as long as possible. We also try to keep them out of court—except, of course, where it's absolutely necessary."

This statement is in sharp contrast with one I read in an article in a magazine by a New York City judge, Jacob Panken, in which he talked about "our brutish teenagers" and advocated bringing more, rather than fewer, youngsters into court.

"No child in trouble was ever hurt by being brought into Children's Court in New York," he said, "or in other states where such courts . . . are established."

At this point, the reader, disagreeing with Judge Panken but remembering a really serious teen-age crime that happened in his area, may well ask: "But what about the vicious young hoodlums who kill innocent bystanders and make the streets of our cities unsafe to walk on?"

The answer is that such hoodlums should be swiftly and severely dealt with—as they are in other countries. Unfortunately, however, such is the increasing efficiency and splendor of our modern communications media that a rape, a killing or a beating (which used to be localized) now is instantly broadcast to every corner of the country, and indeed the world. It creates the impression that such things are the rule rather than the exception.

The fact is that statistics show that this kind of violence is quite small when we consider the problem as a whole. Also, surprisingly enough, violence is one of the easier things to control—through gang workers and other means. Infinitely more serious, and far more difficult to control, is a subtler kind of delinquency—a creeping breakdown of the usual informal restraints, with a resultant misbehavior that is not particularly violent but which is poisonous enough to catch hold of large segments of our youth and turn a fifth of the males into actual court cases. This is the kind of delinquency that many thoughtful people in this country, and just about everybody else in low-delinquency countries, believe can best be handled by playing it down rather than by playing it up, by an expectation of trouble rather than an expectation of good behavior, and by a realistic approach rather than one of indignant alarm.

In many countries, authorities have come to the conclusion that a get-tough approach—a war on delinquents of the type Judge Panken recommends—doesn't work. In Lille, France, for example, a judge decided to crack down on delinquency and organize an all-out drive. The result was that delinquency spread like the Asiatic flu. It soared four times the normal rate in a few months. Finally, the judge called a halt to the drive. Almost immediately, delinquency subsided.

In France, the authorities have decided that the best approach is not a dramatic drive or crack-down, with attendant publicity for the officials concerned, but a muted attempt to get at the seat of the trouble. And one of the first things to do, they feel, is to take a fresh look at the creatures involved. Pierre Morelli, of the French Ministry of Justice, declares that one of the things to remember first is that the adolescent is half-man and half-child—"a creature of romance, passion and impulse"—and should be treated as such. The French, for example, take care to see that he can participate in adult society at an earlier age than ours, as we shall see, but they are also careful not to arouse his young passions and impulses unduly and unnecessarily.

I found it interesting that in France so many of the juvenile judges are young—young enough to remember the transgressions of their own childhood. One of them—Mlle. Nicole Outin, a lovely, blond, poised lady in her early thirties—startled me by her looks and youth. One doesn't expect to find such things in an American judge, and I told her so. She laughed. Apparently such reactions are usual from Americans. But the French see nothing incongruous in having intelligent, attractive young people as judges of their youngsters.

Mlle. Outin, incidentally, had just made a trip across America studying our delinquency problem, and I asked her about her reactions. They were not so different from Dr. Lutz's.

"How many times did I hear people in the United States say, 'You've got to punish them!' " she sighed. "I found the attitude of judges, probation officers, educators, social workers and others quite punitive on the whole. They would say children had done something bad and must be punished. In France, we believe it's not the child's fault. He's been badly brought up. *And one must help him to become an adult.* Not everybody feels that way here, of course, but at least those in charge of our wayward youngsters do." She also found the French family stricter than the American one, with the father having far more authority in the household.

These words were also echoed by Mrs. Tara Ali Baig, of the Council for Child Welfare, in India, another country with a low delinquency rate. She too had just returned from a tour of the United States, where she found the official attitude toward youngsters in trouble far too hostile. "In India," she said, "we think of delinquents as children in need, rather than as offenders."

Such sentiments, of course, are the historical basis of our own approach to the problem—the sentiments that led to our founding the first children's court in the world (in 1899) as well as the first child clinic (1907). But somewhere along the line, the theoreticians moved in, confusion reigned, and our basic approach got derailed. This does not mean, however, that there are not many people in this country who are fully aware of the nature of the problem and would like to do something about it.

Russell Hogrefe, for example, executive director of Chicago's Youth Centers, feels that the elaborate machinery we have created to deal with kids in trouble has become top-heavy and impersonal. He feels that the warm touch is lacking. Dealing daily with youngsters, he has come to the conclusion that when the latter come in contact with the law, they are far more apt to get punishment than rehabilitation.

On the day I was interviewing him, for example, he had just returned from court, where he had secured the release of a fifteen-year-old boy who, although completely innocent, had been held three days in jail as a possible suspect in a South Side robbery. The youngster, incidentally, had received only one meal during the three days of his lockup—a bologna sandwich—and Hogrefe was bitter about our administration of justice. "The only lesson that kid learned from our system of law," he stated, "is that you don't have to be guilty to be punished!"

Dr. Preston Sharp, the director of Philadelphia's Youth Study Center, a place where children are temporarily lodged for "delinquency," although not necessarily for misbehavior, says that the question visitors ask most often when going through the Center is: "Why don't you punish the children who are received at the Center?"

It is not surprising, of course, that the public, fed on a steady diet of teen-age crime minutely reported by the press, radio, TV, the movies and other media, has become alarmed. This alarm, in turn, has been transmitted to the official agencies dealing directly with the miscreants—the police and the courts. Instead of curbing delinquency, this tends to promote it.

Consider what happened not long ago to a young friend of mine in a typical American city—Portland, Oregon. Geoffrey Baldwin, a tall, nineteen-year-old, normally quiet youngster of Quaker background from Stockton, New Jersey, has been attending Reed College for the last several years in Portland, studying engineering. After a hard week of exams, he and two young married couples he knows, also students, decided to celebrate by going to an all-night movie. When they got out in the small hours of the morning, they were full of high spirits and several bottles of beer. They all piled into Jeff's old station wagon. As Jeff pulled away from the curb, one couple decided they wanted to be in the front, the other in the back. Instead of stopping and getting out, they decided to climb over the seats. There was a good deal of laughter, horseplay and pummeling. Jeff drove off, and everybody went home except Jeff, who went to the house of one of the couples to spend the night.

They all slept late, and when Jeff awoke, he was amazed to find he was front-page news. He was also the subject of a city-wide manhunt. The police had been unable to find him in his room, and the dean of the college had already called his parents three thousand miles away. Reading the various news stories, gentle Jeff found himself described as a teen-age hoodlum, the driver of a "getaway car," an abductor, the possessor of a knife, an instigator of a riot and, in one case, his color was even changed from white to black. (He had been wearing a dark ski parka over his head.)

Under the circumstances, everything was understandable, of course. Not long before, there had actually been a killing, and people were, to put it mildly, jittery. An older couple, passing along the street and seeing the melee in the car as it sped away with Jeff at the wheel, called the police and gave them the license number. Between the police and the press, the incident emerged as a full-blown thriller. Eventually, of course, things were cleared up to everybody's satisfaction. The only aftereffect was a few residual shivers along Portlanders' spines, conditioning them for the next "act of delinquency."

Of course, if the police *had* come along while Jeff and his friends were fooling around, things might not have ended so happily for him. Especially if he happened to live in a poor neighborhood. Police are just as sensitive as other officials to the public mood, and they take their cue accordingly. Let me offer as an illustration the experience of a welfare worker I know in Chicago.

This young man was walking along the sidewalk of one of that city's slum sections, where he worked, when he noticed a Negro boy and girl he knew sparring with each other with open hands. They were across the street, and to a casual observer they might have looked as though they were seriously fighting. While he watched, a police squad car came to a sudden halt, a cop jumped out, grabbed the boy by the neck and threw him into the squad car with such violence that he hit his head. A friend of the boy, standing nearby, was outraged at such brutality and challenged the policeman. "Do you have to treat him that way?" he asked. Angered by such interference, the policeman threw the friend into the squad car too. And before the welfare worker could make any protest, the car sped off to the station house.

My friend followed, and his testimony eventually brought about the release of the two boys, who had committed no crime in the first place. Such things happen far more frequently in lower-class neighborhoods than in middle-class ones.

The fact is that, sensing a climate of hostility, police chiefs feel that the popular, and safe, approach is the get-tough one. Unfortunately, the get-tough approach turns out to be the soft, or unrealistic, one.

In San Francisco not long ago, a middle-aged and dedicated layman called Carl May decided to conduct his own campaign against juvenile delinquency. One of the things he noticed in talking with gang leaders was that there was an enormous amount of misunderstanding between them as to what each wanted. He therefore decided to get them all together and have a "beef session" in which everybody could talk out his grievances.

The leaders of twenty-four gangs came. Carl May is a man of strong religious faith, and he insisted on starting off the meeting with a moment of quiet worship. Everybody joined in. Afterward, the boys blew their tops about what they thought was wrong with the other gangs and particularly what was wrong with the police. The latter were blasted in the language of one young leader as follows: "They don't want us in the recreation centers, they don't want us on the streets, they don't want us hanging around the soda fountains. Where the hell do they want us? Home watching TV? We're too old for TV and too young for the bars. We get tired of just hanging around and we *have* to let off steam—even if it means fighting, stealing cars, breaking windows. They think we're all bad, some kind of punks."

Reporters were present, and the next morning, the *Chronicle* carried a front-page headline: "Twenty-four Tough Clubs Meet To Plan Teen Peace." Shortly afterward, a police officer stormed into Carl May's office. He said the captain had read the story and was ready to hit the ceiling. "What're you guys trying to do, start a war?"

he asked. Any sort of assemblage, in his opinion, was just asking for a riot, and he was against it. May, he said, had just been lucky.

May's plans were considerably curtailed as a result, but he did manage to organize many of the youngsters into a loose organization called the Council. Not long after, the Council, with some nudging from May, felt that more legitimate channels of fun should be open to them than those already existing, and they decided to hold a dance. Again the police hit the ceiling. This time May, with the backing of an adult committee, went ahead with plans, hired a hall, and posters went up around town.

A few days before the dance was to be held, two police officers visited Mr. May in his home and cited an ordinance which prohibited any youth below eighteen attending such a function unless accompanied by an adult. They said they planned to arrest anybody violating the ordinance. Next day the newspapers carried front-page stories with the picture of San Francisco's chief of police frowning at the dance posters.

After a good deal of pleading, the chief agreed to allow the dance to be held if: (1) admission was by written invitation; (2) at least fifty adults were present; and (3) the adults would take responsibility for transporting the boys and girls to and from the dance.

Another flurry of front-page stories appeared, as well as editorials congratulating the police on changing their mind. And eventually, in spite of all roadblocks, and with more than a few people holding their breath, the event took place. Present were uniformed and plain-clothed police, reporters, photographers, adult chaperones—and, almost incidentally, the boys and girls, who behaved perfectly. There was only one mishap during the entire evening: a policeman lost his badge!

Not all police are so obstructionist toward young people, of course. And when they do decide to do something about changing kids' attitudes toward them, they find the kids more than eager to cooperate. Right across San Francisco Bay, for example, the city of Oakland has organized a unique police department that could easily serve as a model for the entire country.

A few years ago, feeling that far too much hostility existed between Oakland youngsters and the police, the latter decided to do something about it. With the backing of the powerful Oakland *Tribune,* they set out to sell themselves to the kids as friends. They circulated pamphlets. They addressed meetings in schools. They talked to parents and local organizations. But more important than just doing a job of public relations, they impressed on the 672 men, who comprised the force, the necessity of treating kids with understanding. Far from viewing the program as one of softness, the press thought it hard-headed.

Instead of taking the least efficient men on the force and making them "juvenile officers"—as so many police forces do—they selected their men with strict care. It became a prestige job. In fact, no man could even be considered for this kind of work unless he'd had a successful record of five years' service. Those selected were given a thorough course in handling children. And when they had finished, they were put in plain clothes rather than uniforms, so that a call by one of them on a delinquent youngster would not easily be detected by the neighbors.

In addition, the Oakland police sponsor a number of athletic programs. They are the only force in the country, for example, that holds a junior Olympics, training potential kids for the real Olympics. They act as judges, timers and coaches.

Unlike San Francisco's police, they *encourage* dances. They attend in plain clothes, and even round up some of the kids for it in squad cars. There is a practical dividend to all this, incidentally, which the police had not expected. On several occasions when teen-agers brought liquor to the dance, they were able quietly to learn the source of the illegal supply and take measures to stop it. Without the dance, they might not have learned who the adult culprits were.

Dividends in behavior have been frequent. One youngster, now eighteen, had been a troublemaker for seven years before moving to Oakland. He'd committed every crime in the book, short of murder, and had done considerable time in training school. Out on parole, he got caught up in the police's athletic program. They got him interested in boxing, and found a gym where he could train free. A year later, he won an important boxing award in the state, and has had no further trouble with the law. His record reflects the general situation in Oakland.

What Oakland has done with its police any city could do, if it wanted. Unfortunately, the public mood is so often tinged with fear that such approaches are hard to sell. The give-'em-hell treatment is more popular. And very often the best plans and the best intentions are wrecked by some senseless and wanton teen-age crime which, when fully exploited in the local press, makes the get-tough approach seem beguiling indeed.

The police, of course, are not the only officials to exhibit hostility toward kids in trouble. The courts share an equal responsibility. Most people have the vague feeling that no matter how a youngster is treated before he gets into court, once he is there, a calm, wise, compassionate justice takes over and he gets treatment of a superior order.

Unfortunately, this is not so. Judges are just as responsive to a community's temper as anybody else, as an incident in my own county seat, Flemington, New Jersey, will illustrate.

Not long ago, two seventeen-year-old boys who live in the neighborhood—Stanley Hedgepath and Kenneth Foster—were idling away a few hours in the Circle Diner. They were not brilliant students, but they'd never been in trouble with the school authorities, and certainly never with the police. Awaiting imminent induction into the Army, they'd quit school three days early. At the moment, they were discussing their future over cups of coffee, and wishing they had the chance to give the town something to remember them by before disappearing into the service. Talk of the Army made them think of that old Civil War monument in front of the church, and suddenly they had an inspiration.

Giddy with the brilliance of their invention (they hadn't had a drink), they jumped into Foster's car and drove to Trenton, where they picked up some paint in Aerosol bombs. They drove back to Flemington and waited till it was dark. Then, when no one was around, they got out their bombs and carefully painted the base of the monument a shocking pink. They had some paint left over, and they applied it to the cannon nearby.

With their mission accomplished—"we *really* painted the town red," said Foster to Hedgepath—they went home and slept like babies.

Unfortunately for them, somebody had seen them drive away in

Foster's car, and several days later, they were arrested by the police. They were promptly hauled into court before County Judge Philip R. Gebhardt, a justice who handles juvenile cases on a part-time basis, as is done in many counties.

The judge was not amused—and far from sympathetic. He called the deed "outrageous," "vicious" and a few other things. Neighbors and friends testified to the boys' honesty and general good behavior, but it did them little good. The boys themselves freely confessed their deed, and their families, taken by surprise, gave no thought to getting an attorney. None seemed needed. After all, the boys admitted their guilt and threw themselves on the mercy of the court.

The "mercy" came swiftly. Although preliminary investigations are generally conducted in such cases, the judge decided to dispense with them. (He explained to a reporter later: "We frequently do this when we know everything there is to know about a case.") Furthermore, he decided to make the names of the boys public, another unusual procedure with minors, as an "example" and "for the public good." This accomplished, he proceeded *to sentence the boys to indeterminate terms in the state reformatory.*

When Bruce Hotchkiss, a local newspaperman, told Judge Gebhardt he was astonished at the severity of the punishment to two teen-agers who had never been in trouble with the law before and had done nothing more serious than what is done every spring on campuses all over the United States, the judge was furious. "Sentences," said Judge Gebhardt, "are not only to punish, but to deter!"

Aside from the severity of the penalty the court took against the young boys, however, one wonders if the public was really/served. One does not know if Judge Gebhardt had ever visited our reformatories or studied their recidivism rates, although he certainly should have. Aside from the fact that the public has to pay for the keep of the two boys at the reformatory at the rate of about $3,000 per year each, making a total of $6,000 the court thus imposed on the taxpayer if the boys remained the average stay of one year, there is the further unhappy statistic *that between 50 and 80 percent of all boys sent to institutions in America return to them and to a life of crime.* In effect, the judge was not only teaching them a lesson, as he put it; he was also sentencing them to a better than 50 percent chance of becoming confirmed adult criminals, with all the attendant expense to the taxpayer, to say nothing of the damage to the lives of the boys.

At the time, the judge made much of the fact that the vandalism to the monument would cost $500 to erase. As things turned out, the monument was cleaned by community volunteers using a paint solvent donated by a local manufacturer and so the whole thing cost nothing. How much more sensible it would have been for the boys to be sentenced to cleaning the monument themselves!

Once again, the reader may say that the Hedgepath-Foster case is a rare and unusual one, but the fact is that such stupidities, in one form or another, occur daily. Milton Rector, head of the National Council on Crime and Delinquency, says flatly, "Our courts are hostile toward children. Although we're part of a great pioneer tradition in which people are expected to have the drive and imagination to do anything, we get incensed when kids become deviate and get into trouble. One wonders if Daniel Boone wouldn't have been a delinquent in our present-day society."

Another long-time observer of the scene, Dr. Preston Sharp, of the Philadelphia Youth Study Center, says, "The basic principle of our democracy—that every man is innocent until adjudged guilty in a court of law—is often overlooked when young people are arrested. With juveniles, there is a tendency to think that arrest determines guilt, and that punishment should be immediate."

Admitting that such injustices take place, however, many Americans still feel that when it comes to generosity—i.e., cold cash—we can stack our record up against anybody's.

Can we?

On a private basis, we may be generous with our kids. On a public basis, we are penny pinchers, especially when it comes to dealing with children in trouble.

Many countries, which have had success in dealing with their juvenile problems and which are far poorer than we are, spend a far greater proportion of their income on the welfare of their children than the United States does. Curious as it may sound, we not only deny a large percentage of our children the kind of official warmth and justice they would get in many other countries, but we also deny them the kind of monetary support they would receive if they were living in such places. As far as children are concerned, one wonders if this is really the land of opportunity.

In Sweden, for example, a country high in delinquency but not from lack of financial support, every child up to sixteen years of age is automatically given $90 per year (paid to the mother quarterly) whether the family is rich or poor. The age may be increased to eighteen if the child remains in school. Although the sum is not princely, it's tax-free. Adjusted for the different purchasing powers of the two countries, the sum might be equivalent to twice that amount in the United States. Furthermore, the generosity of Sweden's taxpayers goes so far as to provide free medical care to *all* children up to the age of seven. After that, a doctor is provided with every school. This approach may be a controversial one, but at least the willingness of the Swedes to make large public sums available for child welfare is not open to question.

In Denmark, where delinquency is low, hundreds of day nurseries are available so that no children need be deprived of care while their mothers are working. Costs are low, with the state paying 45 percent, the city 35 percent, and the parents 20 percent. In Copenhagen alone, a city of approximately a million people, there are 257 leisure-time clubs supported by the government for children between the ages of seven and fourteen. A third more are supported privately.

In Austria, a comparatively poor country but one where children are well cared for and the delinquency rate is negligible, the city of Vienna spends 4 percent of its entire budget on child welfare, excluding schools. Stockholm spends 8 percent. New York, our principal city—and possibly the richest in the world—spends *1.6* percent on child welfare, excluding education.

In the Far East, tiny Thailand spends almost a third of its national budget (30 percent) on education alone. Even in Russia children seem to be especially catered to. In Moscow, for example, I found the state supporting five legitimate theaters solely for children.

Let us further consider some over-all figures. In the last decade, Americans spent approximately $78 billion on public education in elementary and high schools. At the same time, they spent $110 billion on new and used automobiles. They also spent $127 billion for recreation, and a whopping $151 billion on cosmetics, alcohol and tobacco!

Against this background of lavish self-indulgence for fun, beauty, drinks, smokes and private transportation, our services for children appear skimpy indeed. Half of our cities (of over ten thousand population) have no juvenile police officers, and half of all our counties have no probation services for juveniles. We have already seen that, like my own county in New Jersey, half of the counties in the country have no special places to detain children except adult jails. In one state, juveniles in thirty counties are still sentenced to the chain gang, and in some they are housed with adult criminals.

Pennsylvania, for example, one of the biggest and richest states in the union, offers only crumbs when it comes to youngsters. As Robert C. Taber, one of the Philadelphia school district's top officials, has pointed out, there are actually seven hundred less beds in Pennsylvania's child institutions today than there were in 1945. At the same time that the final mile of a Philadelphia expressway was being built at a cost of $12 million, the legislature was giving rough going to a bill for $756,000 to improve its services to youth. It was still not passed when this book went to press.

"We haven't had more than the cost of a quarter of a mile of superhighway to spend on capital construction for our children in this state in fifteen years," says Taber.

Although America is the symbol of plenty to people abroad, the plenty seldom seeps down to kids in trouble. In April of 1961, the Philadelphia *Bulletin* carried a story of a thirteen-year-old boy who had been staying in the city's Youth Center for 680 days. The boy had been ordered sent to a state hospital after a psychiatric examination almost two years before, but there was no room for him, and he stayed on at the Center despite the fact that the Center is equipped to hold children an average of twenty-one days. He may still be there now.

In America, social workers, probation officers and others who work with children are among the most poorly paid in the country. Philadelphia, for example, which has openings for twenty social workers at the moment and cannot fill the jobs despite wide unemployment, has a *top* salary scale of $5,877 for them. Starting salaries are much lower ($4,897), although applicants are required to have master's degrees. It is small wonder that people who work with children do not stay in the jobs long: they cannot afford to. Yet nobody high up finds it important to pay them more.

Because of conditions like these, a distinguished educator like Dr. William C. Kvaraceus, of Boston University, feels that youth in trouble in this country "live on a busy two-way street of hate and hostility."

"Like the hard of hearing and the polio victim," he declares, "they too need our help."

In addition to being short-changed in getting help, our delinquents are commercially exploited via the printed page, the TV screen, the movies. In reviewing a Hollywood film about juvenile delinquency recently, *The New Yorker* magazine wrote: "There is something shabby, if not downright indecent, about the use of juvenile crime purely for melodramatic effect, and there is something just as shabby about enjoying it."

Along similar lines, Dr. Kvaraceus said, "Many adults smack their lips as they read the headlines and retell the tall tales of the daring and sexually aggressive acts of the young. Catching themselves in the act, they [the adults] develop feelings of guilt which may then be projected onto the very same youth who got them started in the first place. Now the community really begins to crack down hard."

In talking to a deputy minister for youth in Austria, a man who had recently visited America, I was given his impression of the United States in the following terms: "So many people in America exploit youngsters without any regard for their welfare. In TV and in the movies, people make profits out of the sins of youth. Aggression is glorified. Furthermore, your advertising emphasizes sex among teen-agers. It tends to create a Lolita complex. Children feel they must live up to the advertising." It is interesting to note, in passing, that this man was the equivalent of a cabinet officer for youth. Almost all countries in Europe, and some in the Orient, recognize the importance of their young people by creating a special ministry at the national level to deal with youth problems. There is no such cabinet post in our country.

In view of what many people call indifference, and what other people call downright hostility, and in view also of our unwillingness to provide adequate facilities for our children despite a willingness to exploit their deviance commercially, it is not surprising that many thoughtful people here and abroad wonder whether Americans are really serious enough about the problem to do anything about it.

"Periodically, the public rises up in righteous indignation about the delinquent behavior of youth," says Taber. "But we can no longer do this in good conscience until we have fulfilled our responsibility to children by providing adequate services. It is high time we stop throwing brickbats at the younger generation and begin laying the bricks that will provide the solid foundation for a bulwark of facilities. Time is fast running out."

Before we talk about bricks and other remedies, however, we should say a few words about one or two other things that aggravate the delinquency disease in this country.

5

The Plague of Prosperity

MRS. Violet Alva, the dynamic Home Affairs Minister in India and one of the few lady cabinet members in the world, was sitting in her cheerful bungalow in New Delhi telling me about her recent visit to the United States. She had visited many cities, and many institutions, and she was convinced that poverty had little to do with delinquency, except to curtail it. "I am sure," she said, "that there is more real security for an Indian child in this country, even in a very poor home, than there is in the United States."

Mrs. Alva is not anti-American. She is a thoughtful, intelligent Indian who knows America well. Nevertheless, her statement might sound incredulous to a Yankee just landed in India. That poor land, whose 420,000,000 people have one of the lowest standards of living on earth, doesn't seem to have much security for anyone, least of all for a child.

"Look at it this way," she said. "India is still largely rural. People live on farms, and the family is a strong economic unit. Everybody lives together—father, mother, grandparents, uncles, aunts. Children are never left alone. They are spoiled—within limits—and they always have someone to run to. Anyway, children are not so concerned with financial security. But they are concerned with emotional security. There's lots of it in our family system."

Mrs. Alva may have oversimplified her case a bit, but she made a valid point: namely, that when a country is progressing—which generally means moving from an agricultural to an industrial economy—there is a period of upheaval. The resultant urbanization, mobility and industrialization are hard on all—especially the children. Mrs. Alva's words made me think of the kind of security that once existed for American children when the country was largely rural, and when big, self-contained family farms were the rule, with large families to talk to, with fields to be plowed, animals to be fed, water to be hauled, wood to be cut, etc. People were born, lived and died on the same farm. Today, only 11 percent of the people in the U.S. live on farms (as against 80 percent in India), and one out of every five Americans changes his place of residence *every year.*

In order to emphasize her point that progress accelerates delinquency, Mrs. Alva cited the example of what had recently happened to a small village in the Indian province of Orissa. There, five years ago, a steel plant was built at Rourkela. The area was completely urbanized and industrialized. Prosperity took over. As a result, delinquency shot up from a virtual zero to one of the highest rates in India. Now the government finds it necessary to build some institutions in Rourkela to deal with the offenders.

Another Indian who is concerned with the problem of progress is D. V. Kulkarni, director of social welfare for Delhi. He feels that as India enters a period of urbanization and industrialization, she will face the same problems that other countries have, especially the United States. "But frankly," he said, "we feel we have an advantage. Developing later, we hope to profit by your mistakes."

Not all people in India, of course, feel that mere industrialization, as we know it, is going to produce the same situation that exists in the United States. Some thoughtful persons think that a little of the rebellion that exists in American youth, the kind that produces both the good and the bad in our society, is necessary to have a real breakthrough in creating a new way of life. "India has a religion that encourages passivity, submissiveness and acceptance of one's fate," said Mrs. Tara Ali Baig, of India's Council for Child Welfare. "This is good for preventing delinquency, but is not so good for progress as we know it."

Progress, I found, was recognized as a major factor in delinquency in almost every country I visited—outside of the United States, which, curiously, may be the country with the most progress. Here, the majority of our social workers, whose influence is strong in determining our delinquency-fighting programs, are convinced that the problem is *primarily* one stemming from slums and other depressed conditions. Abroad, the experts consider the idea naïve. They abandoned such notions years ago.

For example, R. J. Whittick, a long-time worker in England's juvenile courts, said, "Twenty years ago, people in Great Britain said that if you could do away with poverty and slums, it would help do away with delinquency. But we've done away with lots of poverty and we've improved housing, and it's worse than ever." Mr. Whittick pointed to a recent survey showing that delinquency rates were higher in new housing developments than in the old slums, a condition that also prevails in the United States.

In West Germany, which has lived through an extraordinary phase of prosperity in recent years, people have come to realize, sadly, that a boom carries a built-in trail of delinquents.

"Germany has had full employment since 1954 and unparalleled prosperity," said Richard Sturm, of the Federal Ministry of Justice, "and yet juvenile delinquency has been unparalleled too. A highly developed society brings many more temptations—more cars to steal, more self-service stores, more material things to long for."

This point of view is especially interesting in view of the study made by Dr. Rudolph Sieverts, of Hamburg's Institute of Criminology, which showed that although the millions of refugees from East Germany are generally in drastic circumstances, their record of juvenile delinquency is far smaller than that of the nonrefugees. "Very probably this state of affairs can be traced to the fact that the refugee families struggle to make up for the external threat to their lives by intensifying their family cohesion," says Dr. Sieverts.

Japan, whose annual rate of economic growth (8.5 percent) is one of the highest in the world, also has, as we have seen, one of the highest delinquency rates. And as Taro Ogawa, one of the country's leading criminologists, pointed out to me, studies have shown that there is actually a close relationship between the amount of money in circulation and the amount of juvenile delinquency.

Another country on the march is tiny Israel. In the process of turning this sleepy little desert land into a vibrant network of roads, factories, housing developments and cities, the Israelis have found themselves with a skyrocketing delinquency problem on their hands. According to Efraim Millo, director of juvenile probation in the Ministry of Social Welfare, the number of arrests of juveniles has doubled in the last ten years. It now stands at 1.27 percent of the juvenile population, which, when corrected for the difference in definition that exists between Israel and the United States, would make the figure approximately as high as, if not higher than, that existing in this country.

Turning again to Sweden, perhaps the most striking example of the relationship between prosperity and delinquency, we see a country which in the words of one of its journalists, Nils Hallerby, "never had it so good." Not long ago, a law was passed there guaranteeing every working person 60 percent of his best annual salary when he retired (up to $6,000 a year). At present, there is full employment (98 percent), no poverty, no slums, health insurance for all, and an astonishingly high order of social justice. If the theory of most of our prevailing experts were correct, namely, that juvenile crime springs from an underprivileged status, Sweden would be a country with little or no delinquency. Yet we know it has one of the highest rates, if not *the* highest, in the world.

Bearing in mind what happens to countries with high prosperity and progress, it's interesting to look again at the other side of the coin—the poor countries. One discovers that in lands that are largely agrarian and nonindustrialized the delinquency problem is relatively nonexistent. If it does exist, it goes unnoticed for lack of agencies to deal with it.

Consider Turkey. Not long ago, General Mehmet Evin, chief of the Turkish national police, boasted in a speech in Canada that his country had no delinquency problem.

"Our police have no trouble with juveniles," he said proudly. "The Turkish family is strong. The children respect the family. They do nothing without parental consent. We have learned a lot about rearing respectful, law-abiding children."

To Americans, with a flock of rebellious teen-agers underfoot, this is alluring talk indeed. And many of us might tell ourselves how pleasant it would be to have children in Turkey.

But would it?

What the general did not say was that to achieve Turkey's state of "bliss" we would have to turn the clock back at least a hundred years. In his land, 80 percent of the population still lives on the land, and not very good land at that. Under such conditions, the family is, of necessity, close-knit. There is very little car-stealing because there are almost no cars to steal, and children don't know how to drive. On the other hand, when children do get into trouble, 67 percent of them are arrested for crimes against persons (murder, assault, etc.). In the United States, only 10 percent of our juvenile crime is of this nature; 90 percent is of a less serious nature.

Another thing the general did not mention is that much juvenile crime goes unnoticed, as it does in many backward countries, because there are simply no agencies to deal with the problem. Turkey has no juvenile court, no probation service, no after-care, no social workers and no school for training such people. What is even more interesting is that when any segment of Turkish youth is given the advantage of youth in other countries, they develop as strong a feeling of rebellion as youngsters elsewhere, as we saw from the student riots that toppled the Menderes government.

A neighbor of Turkey—Iran—is another country which boasts of a low delinquency rate. It also has a low rate of social and economic progress. Youngsters are busy at twelve making camel saddles in the bazaars, and the legal age of marriage for girls is fourteen, although many marry earlier with their parents' consent. There is little time or opportunity for getting into trouble.

However, a man like Dr. Hassein Banai, secretary general of the Council for Youth Guidance, doesn't view his country's lack of delinquency as anything to be particularly proud of.

"We don't have your delinquency," he admitted, shaking his head, "but I frankly don't know which system is more sound—whether it is better to have your delinquency and your way of life or our lack of delinquency and our way of life."

In view of the situation in the countries just mentioned, it is not surprising that the United Nations, following a London conference on the subject in 1960, summed up their findings in a report which said, somewhat grudgingly: "The existing data suggest that the improvement of living conditions—what is called a better standard of living—does not necessarily . . . reduce juvenile delinquency." Another part of the report stated: "Although statistical data are incomplete, it would seem . . . that juvenile delinquency is not caused by poverty or poor economic conditions alone."

Certainly, an objective look at American statistics might give a thoughtful person some reason to say "amen" to these findings. During the Depression of the thirties, our delinquency rates dropped noticeably, and then picked up again during the years of World War II. They dropped again during the transitional recession. In 1948, they began to climb steadily again as our own prosperity increased. High delinquency rates follow upward surges in the economy.

Although the prevailing mood in this country among the social scientists is still one inclined to make poverty the cause, rather than the deterrent, of delinquency—and most of our antidelinquency programs are geared accordingly—it is only fair to say that a few people in the field are beginning to express doubts.

Dr. John Otto Reinemann, director of the Philadelphia County Court's probation, recently took a trip to Germany and England, and came back with the statement that prosperity—"a drive for more possessions"—seemed to be a leading factor in causing delinquency.

Mrs. Katharine B. Oettinger, chief of the Children's Bureau, has also expressed doubts concerning the theories prevailing in this country. Pointing to recent studies that have been made, she said that it appeared that delinquency "could not be proved as resulting from poverty, poor housing or even lack of recreational facilities.

"Delinquency," she added, "is more likely to increase in a time of prosperity than in a time of depression. This seeming paradox makes us question whether the present high rate of delinquency may be a consequence of the social phenomena of our affluent society, the mobility of our population and the rootlessness it produces, the deterioration of our sense of values when everything comes so easily."

Such voices as these, however, are small ones, crying in the wilderness.

Moreover, voices are equally faint when it comes to questioning another notion dear to the hearts of U.S. social theoreticians. This is the idea that delinquency is more or less exclusively a phenomenon of the lowest economic class—in urban slum areas. They refuse to believe that the middle-income or upper-income group is involved in any but a fringe way.

Here again my first clues that all might not be right about this theory came from abroad. Sweden, of course, was the first obvious chink in the sociologists' armor. In that country, the authorities recognize delinquency as exclusively a *middle-class* phenomenon. Why, I wondered, should it be so different in the United States?

Japan added more doubts. In Tokyo, the Classification Center, which processes more delinquents than any other place in the country, finds that 35 percent of all juvenile crime (excluding traffic offenses) comes from middle- and upper-class homes. This is a startlingly high figure when we consider that, in general, the higher the economic level of the family, the easier it is to hide delinquency.

Shortly before I arrived in Japan, for example, I read of a case involving thirty-five Japanese junior high school students who had organized themselves into a highly effective shoplifting team. In another case, twenty-four high school students had organized a group which committed multiple rapes. Japan calls such wayward youth its "sun group," recognizing their privileged status.

In Turkey, shortly after General Evin made his speech extolling the lack of delinquency in his country, I found Istanbul still buzzing over a scandal in which thirty-five upper-class Turkish school girls had been caught red-handed pilfering a safe in which final exam questions had been put for safekeeping. Slightly earlier, in a resort city in wholesome little Switzerland, I found everybody upset because the son of the local police chief and the son of the leading psychiatrist had set fire to their private school, thereby depriving other children of months of education while the institution was rebuilt.

Even Russia, in its rare moments of admitting juvenile delinquency, labels the offenders as children of middle-class families. When I was in Moscow, the papers were carrying an account of cheating on examinations among well-to-do youngsters in Kiev. The article ended up asking the plaintive question so often asked in capitalist countries: "Where and when has our society slipped up?"

In this country, there is plenty of evidence that juvenile misbehavior cuts right across the board of economic and social classes, although it does not show up as such in official statistics.

Not long ago, in New Jersey, there were two revelations of rampant middle-class delinquency within one week—revelations that should have blown sky-high the idea that the problem can best be handled by concentrating on the urban, underprivileged groups in slum neighborhoods.

In Englewood, a dozen boys between the ages of fifteen and seventeen—mostly from wealthy and socially prominent homes—were arrested for taking part in a series of burglaries that netted them $3,000 in a month. The boys, plotting their crimes in a local recreation center, said they stole "for kicks." Many were athletic stars in the local high schools.

A few days later, in Clark, seven boys and three girls—all from "comfortable, middle class families," according to the news account —were arrested for committing eighty thefts over a period of almost a year. "They just took for the thrill of it," said Detective Sergeant Arthur Miskin. "They gave the money away or bought a few items of clothing which they didn't need."

In fashionable Piedmont, California, a suburb of San Francisco, a group of upper-middle-class youngsters had a club whose initiation consisted of stealing something from another car for the youngster's own car. And in a white-collar neighborhood outside Washington, D.C., there was a series of recent automobile thefts in which every car stolen turned out to be one taken by a kid in a middle-class family.

Such delinquents frequently are bored with *just* stealing cars. They demand some new refinement to the trick. Consequently, in one of Philadelphia's better suburbs, a group of well-to-do youngsters developed an ingenious twist: a car-stealing lottery. The game was played as follows: Each day the kids in the group stole a certain number of automobiles, after each youngster had kicked in a certain amount of money for the "privilege" of doing so. Then, at night, when the police announced over the radio the license numbers of the stolen cars, the kid who had stolen the car that was mentioned first took the day's pool.

Often, middle-class delinquency has more sinister aspects. Several years ago in New York's Westchester County, one of the wealthiest neighborhoods in the world, the community was rocked to find that 151 of its youngsters, between the ages of thirteen and nineteen, were involved in taking heroin or marijuana.

In discussing the story, the *Saturday Evening Post* pointed out that Westchester County had organized more social activities, more public and private beaches, swimming pools, golf courses, parks and other recreational facilities to keep teen-agers out of mischief than almost any community in America. Yet, said the article, this problem "has invaded families which have given their children everything that money can buy, every opportunity that schools, churches, and social welfare can provide."

The fact that delinquency runs through all strata of society, without being the exclusive characteristic of any one group, was given statistical support recently in a study made by James F. Short, Jr., F. Ivan Nye and Virgil J. Olson. Of 2,350 high school boys and girls examined in half a dozen Western and Midwestern communities, the researchers found "no significant difference in delinquent behavior in the different socio-economic strata."

"Estimates of the extent of delinquent behavior in the general population indicate that the problem may be more evenly distributed in the various socio-economic strata than the official records lead one to believe," concluded the study.

One reason, of course, why delinquency appears to be primarily a lower-class phenomenon is that the concentration of services is in such areas.

"All social workers work in minority, lower class, urban groups, and so they tend to be impressed by the fact that young delinquents come from this group," says Aaron Schmais, New York's Youth Board official who recently made a survey of gangs for the U.S. Senate Subcommittee Investigating Juvenile Delinquency.

Another reason for the theory is that in lower-class areas a juvenile is much more quickly picked up for an offense than a youngster would be in a middle-class neighborhood. This tends to weight the statistics heavily at the lower end of the economic scale. "In East Harlem," says Schmais, "the label of a delinquent is quickly pinned on a kid—for playing hooky, for stealing fruit, for unlawful assembly, for staying out late."

In support of this statement, I thought of what happened in my own community. A youngster of good family stole a sport shirt from a local clothing store. The store owner knew the father, and that evening he called him up and asked if he should put the item on the bill. The theft, of course, was handled unofficially and never became a statistic, as it might easily have in a lower-class community.

There is evidence of this sort of thing in all parts of the country. Stephen Holeman, of the Los Angeles Probation Department, pointed out to me that kids who violated curfew in privileged Beverly Hills were taken to their homes by the police. Those who violated curfew in underprivileged East Los Angeles were taken to police headquarters.

In New York City, 98 percent of all kids arrested are handled formally in court. In neighboring, wealthy Westchester County, 45 percent of all arrest cases are handled informally—by probation officers, social workers and others—without going through the courts.

There is no doubt that the law is more favorable, the world over, to those living in more privileged strata. "If two persons on different economic levels are equally guilty of the same offense, the one on the lower level is more likely to be arrested, convicted and sent to an institution," according to the late Edwin H. Sutherland, well-known criminologist.

How this works for juveniles was vividly illustrated in a study made in Fort Worth, Texas. Austin L. Porterfield found that a large percentage of college students in the area had committed delinquent acts with impunity—acts as serious as those which brought other young people, less fortunate economically, into court. For example, 43 percent of the college students he interviewed had been truants, and 15 percent had run away from home. Yet *not one* of them had been arrested!

On the other hand, these two offenses—truancy and running away

from home—accounted for 43 percent of *all* the boys brought before
the courts in this same Fort Worth area! Furthermore, Porterfield
found that thefts accounted for 27 percent of all the boys brought to
court, whereas *half the college students admitted thefts of one kind
or another without ever getting caught.*

Statistics, therefore, give one ample *apparent* reason for believing
that juvenile delinquency is a by-product of our lower-class culture.
And this trap seems to be one that the social scientists have fallen
into. Moreover, once committed to a theory, experience has shown
that it is difficult to woo the experts away from it. Their jobs, their
research, their interests make them stick to it.

The public, however, is committed to no such vested interests,
beyond that of keeping their children out of jail. And if they weigh
the facts carefully, both here and abroad, it may be possible to approach the problem from a less lopsided point of view. If the public,
which pays the bill for delinquency through taxes, realizes, for
example, that it's not so much a *class* problem as it is an *age* problem
—*closing the gap between childhood and adulthood*—the road may
be a lot clearer for an all-out, realistic attack on the situation.

The closing of this child-adult gap, of course, is enormously complicated in countries where life has been greatly accelerated by what
we call progress. When a whole new generation of children, for example, is able to own, or at least drive, automobiles, this sudden
change in our way of life is bound to create new mobility, new values
and new sets of problems.

For it is not so much the progress and prosperity that cause delinquency as it is the sudden shifts which such things invariably bring
into people's lives—the breakup of a traditional way of living, the
moving about, the separate homes for various members of the family,
the increased leisure, the lessened need for children to work, the impact of high wages on those who've never had them before, the
inevitable concentration on material things and the equally inevitable loosening of family ties.

In short, *change* is the catalyst. The swifter the change, the more
acute the situation. Settled communities—even tight groupings of
Negroes or Chinese or Jews in what we don't like to think of as
ghettos but which in reality fit this description—have values and

controls which have long been established. Such areas, although considered "underprivileged," don't begin to have the delinquency problem that communities do which are breaking up or which are newly established. Not only in this country, but in a good part of the rest of the world, the old communities are breaking up and becoming something different. Confusion is inevitable, and the effect on the young is disastrous.

"So long as our society is in flux, we can look forward to a high incidence of delinquency and crime," says Dr. Henry McKay, cofounder of the Chicago Area Project.

If one bears this in mind, however, and makes realistic plans to cushion the sudden changes, the confusion *can* be controlled. But generally it takes a while to become accustomed to the new order. "Industrialization and urbanization increase delinquency until society adapts to it," says Dr. McKay. "There's a lag." And the lag, as we have seen, brings with it a good deal of public hysteria.

Certain nations have handled that lag more effectively than others —nations fortunate enough to have a high degree of progress as well as a low degree of juvenile delinquency. The specific ways in which they have achieved this will be looked at in Part II of this book. But at this point, it may be said generally that they laid the ground work for their success by first recognizing the problem for what it is, not something which people would like it to be. In essence, they have started at the beginning, by calmly looking at children as they are—impulsive, emotional, semiadult creatures *longing to be full adults.* They know these creatures cannot be fixed on slides, captured on IBM cards, or theorized about endlessly as though youthful behavior were an exact science, like mathematics or physics.

One thing everybody admits: progress is here to stay. Even among those nations which have not handled their "lag" successfully— nations which are nonetheless plunging headlong into the modern industrial age—I found none which were willing to turn the clock back.

Perhaps the most striking example of this attitude was in Japan, where the able young public prosecutor, Haruo Abe, who has studied in the United States, summed up the Japanese point of view for me.

"Before the war," said Abe, "the military way of life absorbed the wilder elements of youth, the more adventurous. It helped control delinquency and other deviant behavior. After the war, the military ideal was abolished and the whole Japanese way of life was overthrown. However, the Japanese don't resent the disappearance of their old, feudal system. They feel this is the price of progress. Being realists, we don't want to rebuild a feudal system; we want to modernize ourselves. We want to catch up with the rest of the world *even if it means having juvenile delinquency.* One pays for a higher standard of living; there is nothing for nothing in this world. And Japan, I may tell you, is willing to pay the price."

Such a hard-headed look at delinquency should pay big dividends in Japan—as indeed it should in any country, including the United States.

6

Myths, Fads and History

Like the belief that poverty, slums and the lower classes are primarily responsible for juvenile crime, there are other myths that grip the experts—and the public—from time to time. In fact, the field of delinquency is as ridden with fads as the field of fashion. And like an old dress, if an old sociological theory is held onto long enough, it's bound to come back into style sooner or later.

One bit of folklore that is always in fashion, of course, is that the delinquency problem is worse today than it ever was. Like lots of folklore, this may be true, but how in the world could one tell?

There is universal agreement that statistics are hopelessly inadequate today—even to make comparisons between cities, let alone states or nations. How much more inadequate they were in the old days—without typewriters, adding machines, IBM cards and, most important, armies of students eager to do "research" in the social sciences! Comparisons are all but impossible. Nonetheless, there are provocative glimmerings from the past from time to time—things that indicate that the battle between youth and age is not entirely new. Consider the following:

"Youth is disintegrating. The youngsters of the land have a disrespect for their elders, and a contempt for authority in every form. Vandalism is rife, and crime of all kinds is rampant among our young people. The nation is in peril!"

This lament could well have come from J. Edgar Hoover—today. Instead, it came from a discouraged Egyptian priest—about four thousand years ago when the country was going through one of its periodic transitions.

Fifteen hundred years later, one might have thought things would have improved a bit. But according to no less a youth authority than Socrates, who lived in an age which was one of the pinnacles of human achievement, things were not much better.

"Children today love luxury," he said in Athens' Golden Age. "They have bad manners, a contempt for authority, a disrespect for their elders, and they like to talk instead of work. They contradict their parents, chatter before company, gobble up the best at the table, and tyrannize over their teachers."

Shifting to our own country, we find that in the "times that try men's souls"—just before the Revolution—the incidence of youthful misbehavior was still causing trouble. In Philadelphia, in 1764, a clergyman, the Rev. Henry M. Muhlenberg, tells of preaching to a congregation wherein the boys were making so much noise that even the deacons couldn't quiet them down. According to the minister, whenever the boys were shushed, they muttered "Go to hell!" "You son-of-a-bitch!" "God damn you!" and other blunt expletives.

"It is really dreadful in this large city," wrote the Rev. Muhlenberg, "teeming with young folks of all nationalities, who are permitted all freedom, [and] no discipline. The laws are too lenient. It's like trying to check horses with silken threads."

Back in Europe, people were complaining about teen-agers just as bitterly. In England, things got so bad following the Napoleonic wars that a vast inquiry was started to "investigate the alarming increase of juvenile delinquency in the metropolis." The researchers found three principal causes of the trouble: (1) parents, (2) education, and (3) want of suitable employment. And in Scotland, Sir Walter Scott was deploring the lack of protection in Edinburgh, where, he said, gangs of boys in their teens roamed the streets at night and knocked down and mugged all who came their way.

By the time the nineteenth century was a third over, our home-grown delinquents were equally bad. Judging by an article written by Archer B. Hulbert, things had reached a state in this country by the 1830's wherein "half the number of persons actually convicted of crime were youths who had not yet reached the age of discretion." If that is so, juvenile delinquency is a good deal less bad today, for our crime statistics show juveniles committing only 12 percent of the total amount.

In the matter of gangs, which many of us tend to think of as a new twist to urban delinquency, we find the previous century could more than hold its own. One hundred years ago, New York's youth gangs terrorized the city. They bore such repugnant names as Plug Uglies, Roach Guards, Swamp Angels, Slaughter Housers, Dead Rabbits and Forty Thieves. (Today, our youth gangs show the current striving for status, using such names as the Dukes, the Viceroys, the Egyptian Kings, the Crusaders, the Templars and the Astoria Gents. Girl gang members are significantly called Debs.) "Along the waterfront, every corner had its gang, not always on the best of terms with the rival in the next block, but all with a common purpose —defiance of law and order," said Jacob A. Riis, in writing about the nineteenth century. "The gang members were American-born sons of English, Irish and German parents. The first long step taken by a half-grown boy fired by the ambition to have standing in his gang was usually to rob a 'lush,' i.e., a drunken man who had strayed from his way, likely enough asleep in a hallway."

In the famous draft riots in New York during the Civil War, the *New York Times* admitted that the rioting had little or no relation to the draft but was "actually a craving for plunder, a barbarous spite against a different race." (In view of the internecine warfare between whites, Negroes and Puerto Ricans today, this has a familiar ring.) In any event, the riots went on for days, with three-quarters of those participating being in their teens. At one point, the rioters were so numerous that it took twenty-five minutes for them to pass a given spot. The police were unable to cope with the situation at all. Eventually the National Guard was called out.

In those days, of course, weapons were different, just as today adult weapons have changed for more violent ones. In the nineteenth century, gangs used bludgeons, brass knuckles, eye gougers and hob-nail boots (for stomping). Today, it's zip guns, knives and sawed-off shotguns.

Things got so lawless in New York in one year (1862) that *10 percent of the entire population of Manhattan Island was arrested.* There is no breakdown by age of those apprehended, and so no one knows what percentage of them were juveniles. However, it is generally conceded that minors played a large role in the riots and other criminal activities of the period, and it is considered likely that a majority of those arrested were still in their teens.

Considering the foregoing record of youthful misbehavior during the last few thousand years, it is not surprising that social historians Negley Teeters and David Matza have said: "It has always been popular for each generation to believe its children were the worst, the most lawless and the most unruly."

It has also been popular down through the ages to believe that each generation has discovered the true deterrent, the true cure for juvenile delinquency. And one of the things I noted in interviewing experts and laymen alike was that people hold especially strong opinions on this subject. In a series of questions which I occasionally put to groups of people—Rotarians, factory hands, nurses, students, prison inmates, white-collar workers, Negroes, etc.—in an effort to determine what people as a whole believed were the causes and cures of delinquency, I observed that, although there was little general agreement about anything, each person held to his own beliefs with unusual tenacity.

Consequently, at this point it might be a good idea to mention some of the most frequently asserted beliefs, as well as to say what we know about the worth or the futility of each comment.

1. *"Broken homes are the cause of most delinquency."*
In a massive study of nine thousand juvenile delinquency cases handled by the Philadelphia court in 1954, Thomas P. Monahan found that broken homes were twice as prevalent among delinquents as among the general population of the city. However, the inference that the broken home is a cause of delinquency has been questioned on several grounds. First of all, it was found that the percentage of *serious* offenders from broken homes was *less* than

the number from intact homes. Secondly, it has been pointed out that any study which examines only court cases has a built-in flaw: when picked up for an offense, the child with an intact family is more apt to be sent back home, whereas the one from a broken home is apt to be sent to a court and, very often, to an institution.

"Putting all the blame at the door of the broken home is a neat, but too easy, way out," says Dr. William C. Kvaraceus, in a report for the National Education Association. "Too often, it becomes a respectable, though tricky, way of psychologically dismissing the youngster who is difficult to diagnose and who needs help that cannot be easily prescribed."

2. *"What we need are more boys clubs, more recreation for kids."*

Although most people would agree that boys clubs and other recreational and athletic facilities are worthwhile activities, there is serious doubt that such things have any influence on curbing delinquency. Strange as it may sound, boys clubs often have exactly the opposite effect.

F. M. Thrasher, in his intensive study of a boys club in New York City, came up with the distressing news that boys who were members of the club had a *larger* number of delinquencies than boys in the same neighborhood who were not members. Even more distressing was the fact that, while 18 percent of the boys studied were delinquent when they first joined the club, after they had participated for a while in the club's activities, *the delinquency figure rose to 28 percent.*

Equally shattering was the revelation, not long ago, that among all the boys studied in a Pennsylvania reformatory, 35 percent were members of the Boy Scouts.

It is not surprising, therefore, that in a recent pamphlet, the Children's Bureau stated: *"Research indicates that providing additional recreation facilities in an area usually does not bring about significant changes in the volume of juvenile delinquency."*

3. *"If more towns would adopt curfew laws, you'd see delinquency fade away into the night."*

When public pressure for action gets strong enough, many communities quickly pass curfew ordinances, despite the fact that courts have cast doubt on their constitutionality and despite the fact that no one can prove delinquency has been reduced in this way. However, many people working in the field feel that curfews are mere legislative gimmicks which do not assure any long-term success in keeping children out of trouble.

In citing the fact that curfew laws have existed for years with scant evidence of any effectiveness, the Children's Bureau has stated: "The most effective curfew is one applied by parents. It can be flexible to meet different circumstances, and children are more likely to obey it."

4. *"Parents should be punished for their children's misbehavior."*
Some states have enacted "parental responsibility" laws. One, for example, enables the owner of property damaged by a youngster under eighteen to collect up to $300 from the parents.

However, most states now give courts authority to hold parents—or other adults—criminally responsible if they contribute to the delinquency of a minor. If the courts want to use this power they can. To impose more specific financial responsibility on parents is considered questionable both legally and socially. To begin with, such an approach assumes that parents are always responsible for the delinquency of their children because of neglect, abuse or failure to control them. Some parents are simply unable to control their children, and some children are simply not controllable.

One boy, who lived in a state with such a parental responsibility law and who hated his father, deliberately did hundreds of dollars' worth of damage to a store front in order to get even with his parent. Such laws put a terrific economic weapon in the hands of rebellious teen-agers.

5. *"What we need to do is get kids out of the cities—into the open."*
This attractive-sounding notion has more basis in fancy than in fact. Much juvenile delinquency is hidden in rural areas because, as we have seen, the same media of communication do not exist to publicize it. Moreover, forces other than official ones often step in to control the situation. Families and friends in the country do what police and courts do in cities. Furthermore, a child can do things in the country with impunity which he can't do in the city. For one thing, he may carry a gun—for hunting—which a boy in the city may not do. In general, too, child services do not exist in rural

areas to the extent that they exist in urban ones, and so the delinquency figures are lower. Nevertheless, many people seriously suggest
that country living is the answer to the problem, despite the fact that
it is no longer practical in our society for masses of people to live in
rural areas.

In any event, as professional children's services reach out into these
areas and workers begin to probe the hills and dales for misbehavior,
they inevitably find it. In 1958, the Children's Bureau reported: "The
increase in delinquency is not limited to the large cities, as is so often
supposed. On the contrary, the increase in 1958 was much greater in
rural courts (11 percent) than it was in the urban and semiurban
courts (6 percent)."

This is true throughout the world. An international observer,
Dan Q. Moloch-Houwer, head of the International Union of Child
Welfare, says, "The idea that for young people the rural areas are
characterized by healthy air and an uncriminal atmosphere is one
that we can quietly drop. Juvenile delinquency is increasing in rural
areas too."

6. *"We should get tough with misbehaving kids."*

Most people who work directly with kids soon realize that getting
tough just doesn't work so well as other methods, except with a
very small fraction of youngsters who are truly delinquent and
happen to be responsive to this particular type of treatment. Down
through the ages, man has resorted to highly punitive methods with
little or no results. In olden days, pickpockets in England became so
prevalent that the nation decided to resort to the supreme penalty—
death. The law had to be repealed. While people gathered to witness
the hangings, pickpockets moved busily through the crowd. Far
from being deterred, the criminals were pleased at such a felicitous
concentration of victims.

In this country, in the early part of the last century, children of
twelve were still compelled to wear balls and chains in prisons, but,
if what we read about the gangs of that period is true, juvenile crime
did not diminish.

Most crack-downs do not deter because they don't get at the real
roots of delinquency. They treat symptoms, not causes. They confuse,
embitter and confirm in crime the youngsters they are intended to

control. For the most part, delinquents act the way they do out of frustration. To punish without taking into consideration the reasons for such frustrations only compounds the problem and accounts for our sky-high recidivism rates in institutions.

7. *"We need more money for everything."*

More money, spent generally on more services for more kids, isn't so effective as it sounds. Many attempts have been made in this direction, but with negative results.

Let us look at one.

In Washington, D.C., a few years ago, a "Maximum Benefits Project" was started under the auspices of the Youth Council. An underprivileged area was selected with a high delinquency rate where school performance and attendance and behavior were far below average. Part of the area was saturated with services as an experiment. All sorts of aid was given to problem children after careful diagnosis—psychotherapy to both children and parents, legal aid, financial help, health services, group activities, recreation facilities, better housing—the whole glowing rainbow of welfare services. Another similar group of schoolchildren in the same area was denied such services, in order to make a comparison.

Several years later, when a follow-up survey was made, two results were noted:

a) From the school's point of view, the attendance, scholastic and behavior records were no different among the group saturated with services than among those who were untouched.

b) From the court's point of view, there were slightly *more* convictions among the former than among the latter.

It seems obvious that a blanket "more of everything" is not the answer. A more selective and sophisticated use of our resources is necessary to check the spread of delinquency.

8. *"There is no such thing as a bad boy."*

This beguiling bit of fiction is frequently heard, often by fund raisers for private charities. It seems to stamp the speaker as a warmhearted, all-understanding lover of children who knows how to get results. Actually, it's a misdirected attempt to pierce to the heart of a problem with a wobbly cliché.

Sad as it is, there *are* bad children, as people who work with them daily will tell you. Dr. Preston Sharp, of the Philadelphia Youth Study Center, is the kind of man who will lean over backward to avoid the punitive approach in dealing with kids, but occasionally he knows it can't be avoided and that sentimentality is a mistake. On one occasion, for example, he recommended that a boy of thirteen years be sent to the penitentiary. The youngster in question had wanted to steal another boy's bicycle and, in order to do so, found it expedient to push the owner into the river, where the latter drowned. The young delinquent went home, ate a hearty dinner and then slept like a baby.

"No bad boys?" asks Sharp rhetorically. "That fellow was a psychopath. The sooner he was institutionalized, the better."

9. *"Delinquency is growing because the number of working mothers is growing."*

There are no conclusive studies to show that children whose mothers work outside the home are more apt to get into trouble than those whose mothers stay at home. In Vienna, as we have seen, 50 percent of all mothers have outside jobs—the highest percentage in the world—and yet Austria has one of the lowest delinquency rates.

Many other suppositions, theories and fancies seize people from time to time, giving them a momentary ray of hope in solving the problem of youth and crime. For several years, for example, one articulate group has been urging better eating habits. It feels food will solve everything. Pointing to a survey of three thousand delinquents that revealed that on the average such youngsters eat only three meals at home each week and further citing the fact that the Chinese (who have a low delinquency rate) stuff their young with fresh vegetables, this group syllogistically concludes: "The best place to solve the problem of delinquency is in the cooking pots of the home."

The experts, of course, generally have a far more complicated approach to the problem than this one. Their theories are elaborately worked out, heavily buttressed with sociological research, and ringed about with impenetrable jargon. The results, alas, can be just as silly.

The trouble, naturally, is that there is a certain amount of truth in most theories. The question is how much. Since the resources with which to fight delinquency are not unlimited, we must put our money and effort into those ideas which promise to yield the biggest dividends. In short, the winners.

Currently, several theories are riding high among the experts and private foundations are betting millions on their validity.

One, for example, stripped of most jargon, is simply that juvenile delinquency is a manifestation of "lower-class culture"—a subculture, if you will, that has a whole set of values which are completely different from middle-class values. This group is characterized by so-called "female-based households," where the father is frequently or entirely missing and where boys are raised in a female atmosphere. The Negro is a good example of this because such households are generally based on a matriarchy, with the men moving on and the women remaining to rear the children. In such families, sociologists tell us, the young boy in seeking his sex role has nothing to identify with. Consequently, he goes outside the home—on the street corner or with the gang—in order to prove his masculinity and toughness.

This theory, however, is already slightly passé, and stands fair to be replaced by an even more modish one—"status discontent." In the trade, this is simply called the "status," or sometimes the "opportunity," theory. "It's big at the moment!" admitted an institution head to me recently. (He has seen many ideas come and go.)

According to the "opportunity" theory, lower-class boys have not had the training and privileges which enable them to cope with such middle-class-oriented institutions as school. They suffer "status deprivation" and "low esteem" as a result. Furthermore, they find that, although middle-class standards are constantly being held up to them via school, advertising, movies and other mass media, when they try to achieve these standards, they discover that most of the avenues of advancement are closed to them. A Negro or a Puerto Rican, for example, finds it harder to get a scholarship or a good job than another boy. Consequently, these boys become part of the delinquent subculture. They try to capture esteem and status in some other way, such as joining a fighting gang and acting tough.

The trouble with this theory is that nobody has explained why, throughout history, certain people arise out of intolerable conditions and others do not. Why, as Sheldon and Eleanor Glueck have asked, should two "Als"—one named Smith and the other Capone—both come out of the same type of slum? There are obviously other factors at work.

Most social scientists, possibly because of their training and background, are inclined to view the juvenile problem as essentially an economic, or material, one. They feel that because some children are less fortunate financially than others, these youngsters are rebelling against society for a larger share of the cake, especially the one with the thickest status icing. Being status-conscious themselves and caught up in a continual scramble for academic degrees and other recognition, they tend to feel that teen-agers must think the same way.

This has not been my experience in talking to the youngsters themselves. Most of them want to be adults all right, and are impatient about achieving this status, but the average delinquent of fifteen or sixteen doesn't feel himself deprived economically—even though he may well be. Children simply don't think about such things the way adults do. They are more apt to be thinking about fun and excitement and impressing their friends, especially by trying to play an adult's role.

In talking to hundreds of youngsters—both delinquent and non-delinquent—I found that the basic things the misbehaving ones were interested in were adventure, change, risk and excitement.

This idea has also been suggested by the Gluecks in their monumental study of five hundred delinquents matched with five hundred nondelinquents—both of exactly the same age, racial background and general intelligence, who also came from the same underprivileged city neighborhoods.

Over and over again, the Gluecks found the delinquents were boys with an "excessive thirst for adventure"—to be exact, 55 percent of the delinquents versus 18 percent of the nondelinquents. In other days, such boys might have gone to sea on whaling ships, fought against the Indians or cut pioneer paths through the wilderness. Today, the same type of youngster, with the same inordinate craving for adventure, is apt to find little outlet for it, beyond watching TV, and he may well end up as the leader of a fighting gang.

In reading the case histories of many youngsters in training schools and reformatories, I was particularly struck by what they said when they were asked to put their own stories down in their own words rather than in the words of the case worker. Curiously, the same phrases would pop up again and again. Such things as "I ran away for the adventure I thought I'd find," or "I couldn't get rid of a yearning for excitement," or "I wanted to live it up fast."

Not long ago, the newspapers carried an account of two Texas boys, fourteen years old, who during one weekend in Houston managed to do $170,000 worth of damage to 153 new foreign cars parked in a distributor's lot. They found a way to start the cars and run them into each other.

Why did they do such a thing?

"We wanted something exciting to do," one boy said. "We thought it would be fun to play around with the cars."

It will also be remembered that in the Englewood and Clark, New Jersey, scandals, involving multiple thefts by high school kids, the explanation given by the teen-agers was that they stole for "kicks" or for "the thrill of it."

None of these youngsters was economically deprived. Nor did they feel they were being denied status or opportunity. They were, however, restless, bursting with energy and longing to act out their conception of big-shot adults.

Of course, many of the schemes suggested by the social scientists are highly desirable. Even the poorest ones have some kernels of merit. There *should* be more equality of opportunity, more recreational areas, more and better housing, better health services, etc. But the important thing is that we should not delude ourselves into believing that these things are going to control delinquency. As a Swedish official in Stockholm said to me, "Clearing slums, building recreation centers, and providing better social services are things that *you do for themselves* to build a better way of life for your people. But we no longer expect that these things have anything to do with curbing delinquency."

Not long ago, a mother with several grown sons—Mrs. Marda Alexander, of Evanston, Illinois—wrote me of her disillusionment with "theories."

Since our older son was born 28 years ago, I have watched a constant shifting of philosophical attitudes about the rearing of children, ranging from the most rigid to the most permissive, with every nuance in between. Every crackpot with a Ph.D. was given the same rapt attention, when he handed down a new theory, that Moses presumably gave to God when he handed down the Ten Commandments. And each time the experts cried triumphantly: "There's the answer!" Only it never was.

Everybody had a panacea. It was thought for a while that more recreational facilities might be the answer. Or that parents were at fault. Or that society had failed.

It seems to me that this futile attempt to oversimplify a most complex situation has kept us from getting to the core of the problem. Maybe if we could wipe the slate clean of all preconceived ideas about delinquency and start from scratch, we might begin to make progress—somewhat the way the atom bomb was built.

Mrs. Alexander has a point. Perhaps we, as a nation, have been too prone to abdicate our prerogatives to the "scientists" and wait for the single nostrum that would solve all our juvenile problems. This has been an easy trap to fall into because the idea has worked well on other maladies, like polio, diabetes and tuberculosis. However, it is beginning to dawn on many people that behavior ills are too complex to respond to a single remedy.

But on another point Mrs. Alexander is wrong. We don't have to "wipe the slate clean and start from scratch." Many of us will have to readjust our thinking, and certainly the public is going to have to assert itself, but the fact is that many sound ideas are already operating both here and abroad—*ideas which can serve as nuclei around which to build an effective delinquency control plan.*

But before we take a look at the successful—and not so successful—remedies being used around us, let's take one quick look at the patient, the object of all our attention: Mister Juvenile Delinquent Himself!

7

THE ADOLESCENT LIMBO

THE core of the American delinquency problem, as we have seen, is the young male, aged fifteen to seventeen. He outnumbers the female delinquent by far, sometimes as much as ten to one. According to the best estimates, one out of every five teen-age boys will get into trouble with the law during the years of his adolescence.

This is a shocking figure. And yet, as one looks into the problem more deeply, the figure doesn't seem high at all, *considering the facts*. Actually, we have placed a large proportion of our youngsters in an intolerable situation. With the best intentions, we have made it more and more impossible for them to grow up normally. Far from helping them become adults, we have hindered them.

Let us try to remember our own childhood. A good deal of time was spent, if we are honest, in longing to be adults and to have an adult's privileges. From time to time, of course, we actually had the delicious experience of playing an adult's role. When America was 50 percent agricultural, a boy played a man's role early and easily, and the transition was not hard. He drove a team of horses, he cut and hauled wood, he plowed, he did all the things a man does as soon as he could. Furthermore, he was an important part of the family economic unit, *and he knew it*. Gaining status as a man was not a problem. It came early.

Even in cities it was not too difficult to achieve the role of an adult. If a boy was not suited to an academic education or he didn't like it, he went to work early. He earned money, even if he was only an apprentice, and money confers status. For those boys who didn't want to do either of these things—the so-called wilder elements of our youth—there was always the West, waiting to be conquered. One wonders how many of our restless, energetic pioneer heroes would have been juvenile delinquents if compelled to live today in our towns and cities with their supermarket, going-steady, button-down-collar culture of the mid-twentieth century.

If we look at all today's prosperity, urbanization and industrialization—which we call progress—it's easy to see how we've created for our youngsters an impossible dichotomy.

On the one hand, we encourage adulthood in the young. We raise them to mature earlier physically. Recent studies in Germany have shown that puberty occurs earlier in prosperous, well-fed populations than in undernourished ones. Consequently, our youngsters acquire the bodies and emotional needs of adults at an earlier age than formerly. Furthermore, although we may not actively encourage early dating and going steady, we condone it at ever earlier ages. We make cars available for them to run around in, and many youngsters can drive them as early as sixteen. Certainly, a large part of our splendid communications and advertising media expose the teen-agers to all the temptations of acting like an adult—in dress, in travel, in dating, in smoking, in drinking, in sex. Living in an affluent society, a child is more aware of the material advantages of being grown up than he has ever been in history.

But, on the other hand, although we hold up this glittering prize of adulthood constantly, at the same time we tell the male teen-ager that he must not really touch it for some time. We withhold the prerogatives of being an adult longer and longer. Although we have not slowed up his physical development (and have even accelerated it), we have not accelerated his chance at adulthood. In fact, we have subjected him to a period of compulsory childhood. We have told him he must not leave school until he is sixteen, and if he does leave then, we have made it virtually impossible, because of labor laws, union policies, insurance and other regulations, for him to get any kind of permanent job until he's eighteen. Because of our unemployment situation, most boys can't get them even then.

Furthermore, if our adolescent male happens to be the kind of boy who is not interested in the type of education our college-oriented high schools offer (and the estimates of this kind of boy run as high as one-third of our juvenile population), then there is no alternative for him in our school system. If he is unable to make the grade in a vocational school or is backward or disinterested, he must nevertheless sit it out in the schoolroom, often the butt of jokes, for years. In most schools, there is no other course open to him. If he gets mad or bored, he can of course play truant or join a gang or drive a stolen car or something else that may satisfy his craving to act the role of an adult..

If he is unfortunate enough to be one of the 20 percent of our boys who actually get into trouble with the police, what then? He is apt to find that Americans are quite impatient with deviant behavior. Believing that we have provided our teen-agers with the highest standard of living any society has ever offered them, we tend to feel they should be grateful. Or, at the very least, not tear up the scenery.

Curiously enough, the fact is that although our living standard may be high many of these best-fed, best-housed, best-automobiled kids *are* underprivileged. In prolonging childhood, in gearing our curricula and our academic standards fairly generally for college, in keeping kids in school and out of work while we simultaneously expose them to temptations no group of youngsters has ever been exposed to before, we have indeed deprived them of the one thing all children need most—help in bridging the difficult gap between childhood and adulthood!

Not only do we deny that help in many cases, but we are demonstrably quicker than any other country to pin the label of "delinquent" on erring youngsters. We subject them to a police that is more often unsympathetic than otherwise, and we tend to prefer punishing rather than rehabilitating our youngsters. In addition, we starve many of the services that could help our delinquents—the courts, the institutions, the juvenile police. We pay our probation officers—whose role is acknowledged to be crucial in rehabilitating a kid—an average of $4,000 to $5,000 a year, while we pay our truck drivers $7,500 to $10,000. And once the probation officer fails (and he's apt to fail because we need thousands more to meet minimum standards), the youngster gets sent to an institution where we make it all but impossible for him to learn much of anything but the fine art of how to become an adult delinquent.

Aside from the delinquents, it's hard, too, for the 80 percent of the boys who *don't* get into trouble—or at least who don't get picked up. If they don't fit our particular type of high school education and drop out, it's difficult for them to find anything more useful to do than watching television. Even the things that used to keep a youngster busy until recently—things like going to the store, or cutting the lawn, or putting the coal in the furnace—have largely disappeared. More and more people shop but once a week and store food in freezers, grass is cut by power mowers, and furnaces are run by oil. Our busy roads make bicycle-riding hazardous, and kids inevitably learn to depend on cars.

In the matter of sex, we expose our kids to plenty of it, more than ever—through advertising and movies and television and other media—and yet we offer them little or no sex education in school. Although there is evidence that children are maturing earlier physiologically, they are expected to defer gratification of sex desires longer. This may be why there has been a 67 percent increase in illegitimate children among teen-agers since World War II.

Coupled with this lack of sex education is the fact that the teaching of ethics has disappeared from our school curricula. Although people abroad, and many here, hold that old-fashioned concentration on the teaching of morality and ethics yields enormous dividends in combating delinquency, most experts, strongly influenced by the psychiatrists, feel that such courses are futile and somehow not quite "modern."

In short, the male adolescent who isn't interested in college is apt to feel there is no place for him in our society—i.e., no legitimate place—during the years I would like to call the Critical Age. Paradoxically living in the most privileged nation in history, he finds that for him the most important privilege of all—proving he is a man

—is denied him. Registering his importance to his family and to the community, and thereby taking his place in adult society, is indefinitely and dangerously postponed.

Consequently, when all facts are taken into consideration, including the crucial one that our definition of juvenile delinquency tends to get broader all the time while the official net gets more capacious, one is sooner or later forced to the inevitable question: Why isn't there more delinquency?

PART II

THE REMEDY

THE REMEDY

8

THE PSYCHOLOGICAL APPROACH

NOT long ago, Florence Sytz, professor of social case-work at Tulane University, who must be the scarred victim of many a juvenile delinquency conference, created a brilliant parody of how to conduct such a conference. Her formula can be, and has been, used equally effectively in writing a book on the subject.

Among her suggestions:

1. Profess not to have the answer. This lets you out of having any.

2. Point out that the deepest minds have struggled with the problem. This implies that it does you credit even to have thought of it.

3. Say we must not move too rapidly. This avoids the necessity of getting started.

4. Say the problem can't be separated from all the other problems. This means it can't be solved until all other problems are solved.

5. For every proposal, set up an opposite one and conclude that the "middle ground" (no motion whatsoever) is the wisest course of action.

6. Discover that there are all kinds of "dangers" in specific conclusions.

Despite such good advice this part of the book will recklessly ignore all these suggestions and plunge headlong to conclusions. It will deal primarily with the various approaches being used to fight delinquency at the present time, both here and abroad, and attempt some sort of evaluation of each—from the public's point of view.

One of the basic approaches to delinquency prevention and treatment is the psychiatric one. And in discussing this, we find we are dealing with an almost exclusively American product. Although we are told that our psychiatric services are woefully inadequate—and they certainly are in many places—the fact remains that other countries have only the merest fraction of this kind of service, if indeed they have any at all. Some nations feel they would like to have it if they could afford it. Others feel that such methods produce meager results.

In Austria, the home of modern psychiatry and Sigmund Freud, the psychiatric approach is used sparingly. "We feel you people have gone overboard on this tack," a Vienna juvenile court judge who recently visited the United States told me. "We use it only in severe cases and in setting up the regime in an institution."

Said an English official in the Home Office: "In training our social workers and probation people, we don't fancy up our courses with a lot of psychology stuff. We feel it might interfere with their native common sense."

On the other hand, I recently asked a young psychoanalyst in a New Jersey clinic what percentage of delinquents he felt needed psychiatric help. His reply was an unhesitating "One hundred percent!"

This answer illustrates the single-mindedness that exists among each separate group of professionals attempting to deal with the juvenile problem. It's a bias that implies there's only one answer. It's also a bias that makes it confusing to outsiders (like Arthur Miller, as we mentioned earlier) when they attempt to learn something about the problem from the experts.

So far as I could learn from comparing notes with people who deal with young offenders at the working rather than the theoretical level, a fair estimate of those who actually need psychiatric help ranges between 5 to 20 percent. Most people (if we exclude psychiatrists) think the figure is closer to 10 percent, or less.

In matching five hundred delinquents with five hundred nondelinquents of similar background and studying them in depth, Sheldon and Eleanor Glueck found only 7.3 percent of the delinquents "psychopathic" as opposed to .4 percent of the nondelinquents. School authorities gave me estimates ranging between 10 and 20 percent, with most quoting the lower figure. Dr. Richard Jenkins, who created the theory that delinquents are either "adaptive" (nonfrustrated in their delinquency) or "maladaptive" (frustrated), believes that there are about 20 percent of the latter and that they need psychiatric help. In general, people who deal with rebellious youngsters on a day-to-day basis in courts, in schools and on the streets feel that the number of those who need this kind of help is relatively small. They feel that the "sick" aspect of delinquency has long been exaggerated.

"A widespread conception of youth who commit violent and serious acts of delinquency is that they are neurotic, emotionally disturbed or in some way maladjusted," says Anthony Sorrentino, head of the Illinois Youth Commission's Chicago Area Project. "Such a conception is misleading and certainly not in accord with the knowledge available. Only a small percentage of adolescents who engage in delinquency are disturbed in the traditional psychological sense." Sorrentino further believes that the incidence of delinquents who have "personality problems" is not likely to be greater than that found in other groups—in a club or on a football team, for example.

His viewpoint is echoed by Judge Reinemann, of Philadelphia's County Court, who says, "Nothing is being gained by saying every delinquent is a sick child. You thus remove the child from a proper understanding of his problem. Psychiatry may be a useful treatment in no more than 10 percent of the cases."

Except for the very rich, who can afford to take their children to psychiatrists and pay the going rate of $15 to $25 per hour, the only resource most parents with problem youngsters have—if they live in a large city or well-endowed community—is a child guidance clinic. Here they pay what they can afford to pay.

Such a clinic can be found in Fairfax County, Virginia, a community a few miles south of Washington, D.C., which I visited not long ago. The area is a typical middle-class, white-collar community where the median income is about $7,500 a year, a figure not so very much higher than the national average. The clinic, presided over by outspoken Dr. James Thorpe, former chief medical officer and psychiatrist at the Federal Training School, is in a pleasant, red-brick building. It takes on youngsters who have been sent by the court for diagnosis and, in many cases, for treatment. Other youngsters, who have not reached the police or court stage, may also come if their parents feel they need help.

In group sessions and singly, Thorpe and his assistants try to solve the delinquency problem by treating the whole family, not just the child. "We have an advantage over institutions," says Thorpe. "We get to work on the parents too." After mother, father and child attend therapy sessions, either singly or in a group, then the whole family gets together for what Thorpe labels "a psychiatric cook-out." They try to thrash out their problems during a verbal cross fire.

The clinic is supported by the community, but parents pay a nominal fee, according to income. Generally, it's one dollar per week for every thousand dollars of yearly income. Thus, if a man earns $7,500 a year, he pays $7.50 a week.

The clinical approach to juvenile delinquency is found in a number of parts of the world, but the concept was started in America in 1909 when Dr. William Healy established one in Chicago for the juvenile court. He suggested that a combination of things—mental, physical and spiritual—was responsible for delinquency and that the combination varied with different cases. Since that time, similar organizations have been set up in large cities—for diagnosis, consultation and treatment. Hospitals, universities, adult education centers and settlement houses have established them, and as time has gone by, they have become more and more psychiatrically oriented, although this was not Dr. Healy's original aim. Today children's clinics are almost synonymous with psychiatry, and they are under increasing fire. Their value in curbing delinquency has been sharply questioned, and there's considerable ground for feeling that their approach has become more theoretical and less practical.

A few years ago, for example, a study was made of the Wayne County Clinic in Detroit by H. W. Dunham. He found that although the number of trained staff members had increased over the years, and was matched by a corresponding decrease in the number of cases each member had to handle, the recidivist rate of young people referred by the court had *not* decreased at all. In sum, the cost of the clinic had gone up, but there was no noticeable impact on the community's juvenile delinquency.

In the most recent report to the Congress, the Department of Health, Education, and Welfare summed up its point of view as follows:

> Several studies have attempted to evaluate the effectiveness of clinical treatment of delinquents. The results of these studies are inconclusive; they have proved neither its effectiveness nor its ineffectiveness. A careful perusal of the literature of psychiatry, psychology, mental health, and the other so-called "helping professions" leaves one with the impression that the *apparent ineffectiveness of clinical intervention in the delinquency process* is due either to the absence of appropriate conditions for therapeutic contact, or the absence of needed health, education, recreational or vocational services once such contact is established.

Certainly no one can say our government sounds wildly enthusiastic about more and bigger clinics.

One can say, however, that clinics have had some usefulness in diagnosis and in treating the comparatively small percentage of youngsters who are seriously disturbed. On the other hand, to look upon them as a major factor in fighting existing delinquency would be a mistake. And to count on them to play a major role in the even more important task of preventing large-scale delinquency would be a greater mistake.

Certainly, clinical and other psychiatrists have rendered a useful service in giving all of us a greater insight into the delicate psychological balance wheel around which the average family revolves. It is true, of course, that in many countries, where psychiatrists do not exist, these things are understood instinctively, but in any event it has been spelled out for us here in that scientific language which our society seems to like and has come to expect from its experts.

One of the most significant ideas which psychiatrists have gotten across to us, for example, is the importance of the "father image" to the average male adolescent. This is a concept which, as we have seen, was crucial in helping the Italian boy, Guido, resolve his prob-

lems when he got into trouble for shooting another boy. The lack of
it was also important in creating such a problem for Fred, the Air
Force major's son.

Dr. Thorpe is of the firm opinion that the American father is at
the root of most juvenile delinquency. Or, in his own words: "The
lack of a strong father image is central to delinquency."

"When a kid comes to the clinic, it often looks as though the
mother is to blame," he says. "She's uncertain. She's hovering. She's
doing all the wrong things. But when you look into it further, you
find she's that way because the father isn't a strong one. And by
'strong' I don't mean autocratic.

"Most fathers of delinquents work hard. They may be active in
church and they may keep the lawns cut, but their relationship with
their sons is bad. They rationalize their nonparticipation in their kids'
activities on the basis of being busy working. And because they're
good breadwinners, they feel they've done their job. Furthermore,
they expect good behavior from their kids. When they don't get it,
all hell breaks loose."

The importance of the father as a key factor in preventing delinquency is recognized in almost every country of the world, whether
there are clinic heads to say so or not. In Germany, the well-known
juvenile court judge in Freiburg, Wolf Middendorff, said, "A boy
learns to be a man by copying his father. If there's nothing worth
copying, the boy soon senses it and turns to other heroes."

In Japan, before World War II the father was a "little emperor,"
with absolute rule in his own home, just as there was a "big emperor"
with absolute rule at the head of the country. There was little delinquency. But the system was feudal in nature and doomed to failure
sooner or later in the modern age. "Unfortunately, we haven't had
time to work out a satisfactory substitute for this system, which is why
we have such a delinquency problem," said Haruo Abe, Japan's public prosecutor.

In Turkey, which has not yet felt the real upheaval of modern
progress and where delinquency is low, or at least hidden, the father
is still supreme. Mrs. Suheyla Kunt, an attractive Istanbul housewife,
who is one of the few people active in child welfare work there, told
me that her father selected her husband for her (an arrangement,

incidentally, which worked well), and that when she was growing up, she was so fearful of her father's judgment that she never did anything without asking herself what he'd think of it. "When I was a child," she said, "I was only allowed to kiss my father's hand on festival days. This still happens in the small towns and villages, but it's changing in the big cities."

Karl-Erik Granath, of Stockholm's Child Welfare Council, believes that one of the reasons for Sweden's swollen juvenile problem is that with the removal of the family from the country to the city the father's role has diminished in importance and that no adequate other arrangements have yet been worked out.

In our country, perhaps the most striking example of the relationship between the loss of father prestige and the male delinquent can be seen among our Puerto Rican population.

As Harrison Salisbury pointed out in his excellent book on gangs, *The Shook-Up Generation,* the father in Puerto Rico, where delinquency is low, is the unquestioned chief of the household. Women are not usually wage earners, and no matter how poor the family, the father is "the responsible and dominating figure."

When the Puerto Rican arrives in New York, however, the role is reversed. The mother often gets a job in the needle trade where wages are good. The father is relegated to a menial job, if he gets one at all—shining brass, washing dishes or pushing a cart through the streets of the garment center. The youngster meets other kids whose fathers are successful, and, in a society where much emphasis is put on material success, like owning a car, a home or a television set, the boy's father image is downgraded to the point of being barely perceptible. As a result, Puerto Ricans here have a delinquency rate out of all proportion to their population and one quite different from that which exists in Puerto Rico.

Does all this mean that mothers should not work?

Not necessarily. Some countries take working mothers in their stride without increasing delinquency, but they do offer other opportunities and services—as we shall see—to take up the slack. And at no time do they forget that, generally speaking, a son learns from a father, and a daughter learns from a mother. In the Gluecks' study of the male adolescent, they found that twice as many of the delinquents as the nondelinquents failed to look upon their fathers as "acceptable patterns for emulation."

In addition to such things as pointing up the importance of the father in our delinquency problem, helping us understand the psychological bases for family conflict, and diagnosing and treating the psychotic youngster, the psychiatrists have provided us with another useful tool in treating young delinquents—group therapy.

This fairly recent technique has been used in clinics, hospitals, prisons and various other places from time to time. But perhaps nowhere has it been used more effectively than it has at Highfields, a small, juvenile delinquent treatment center near Hopewell, New Jersey. Located in the old Lindbergh house, where the famous kidnaping took place a quarter of a century ago, Highfields has been operating successfully for more than ten years. It is worth looking at because it's an example of a treatment that works well with certain types of delinquents and because, as so often happens in this country, its success has attracted few U.S. imitators.

Highfields was built on the idea that much could be done with boys who were not too far gone in delinquency if they were given a chance to live in homelike surroundings, work at something useful during the day, and have an opportunity at night to thrash out their beefs in bull sessions. The latter are, of course, not called bull sessions. The directors, in the turgid terminology of their profession, call them "guided group interaction sessions." The boys call them simply the "meetings."

One of the important features of Highfields is its smallness. It takes only twenty boys. They live in a big house with no locks, no guards, no fences and no uniforms. The atmosphere simulates the normal world as nearly as possible. The boys work an eight-hour day, five days a week. They do unskilled jobs at a nearby mental institute, for which they are paid fifty cents a day. When they come home after work, they eat a dinner cooked by a motherly woman with the improbable name of Mrs. Moonlight. Soon after dinner, they divide into two groups and go to the two-hour "meeting."

Sessions are held five nights a week. Attendance is not compulsory, and sometimes the new boy doesn't go. However, by the grapevine he soon learns that the "meeting" is the way to work one's way out of Highfields, since a boy's sentence is indeterminate and he is released when the director—*and the boys*—feel he has solved his "problem." At the beginning, he is often reluctant to talk about himself or others in the "meeting," but sooner or later he gets caught up in the provocative, no-holds-barred sessions, and he generally ends by talking his head off. The "meetings," incidentally, are as sacred as a confessional. No information revealed in them is used against a boy. The language is direct and the anecdotes eye-popping.

At first, a new boy tries to present himself in a sympathetic light. But the other boys, who've been at this sort of thing for several months, are quick to spot humbug, and say so in the earthiest way possible. After a while, the boy gets the idea that if he isn't honest with his peers (and with the director, or assistant director, who presides over the meetings), they won't think he's solved his problem and is ready to go home. Eventually, he comes clean. In the process, he begins to see himself as he really is, aided and abetted by the others. Usually he's surprised to find that the problems of another boy are as bad as, or worse than, his.

The center's first director, Dr. Lloyd McCorkle, feels that the crux of Highfields' success is the ruthless honesty it elicits in the meetings, which, in effect, is not so different from what takes place in a gathering of Alcoholics Anonymous.

"Most juvenile delinquents blame others for their plight," he says. "They blame judges, police, politicians, parents, bad companions. At Highfields, they learn to blame themselves—the first, painful, crucial step in rehabilitation."

Let us look for a moment at what happened to a single boy at Highfields, an Italian youngster from the tough streets of Newark. We'll call him Dino. A mugger, a thief, a vandal and an artist at other criminal acts from the age of ten, he landed in Highfields at sixteen. A lone wolf type, he kept away from the meetings, until one night he decided to go "just for the hell of it." There wasn't anything else to do.

He went every night thereafter, but he was a surly and silent attendant. He still continued to steal food and clothing from the other boys whenever he could. One night, in a meeting, Dino listened while a new boy announced his jacket had been stolen. The

director, who was presiding, and some of the boys suspected who
had stolen it, but no accusations were made. Finally, one of the
boys suggested everybody chip in and buy the new boy a jacket. At
this point, Dino slipped out of the meeting. A few minutes later, he
came back and tossed the jacket into the owner's lap. "I took it," he
said simply.

Nothing at all was said about the incident—then or later—but it
turned out to be a turning point in Dino's life. He stopped stealing,
and several months later he left Highfields. After a while he found
a job as a salesman and got married. Today, in his mid-twenties,
he is a success. The energy and aggressiveness which made him the
scourge of his neighborhood and which are now legitimately channeled earn him an annual income in five figures. Even more essential
to his success, however, is the fact that in his spare time he spends
hours as an unpaid volunteer worker with delinquent boys. He knows
all the angles and all the pitfalls. The local probation officer considers
him an invaluable assistant.

What psychologists believe to be the essence of Highfields' therapeutic technique is that it takes a boy's instinct to be part of a group,
or a gang, and instead of the gang working *against* his best interests,
it works *for* him. I have sat in on many of these gang sessions at
Highfields, and I am amazed not only at the naked objectivity with
which boys discuss their shortcomings but also at the *esprit de corps*
which develops when boys try to help each other solve their problems.

Not all boys at Highfields succeed, of course. A small percentage
run away or are so difficult to manage that they are returned to juvenile court and reassigned to Annandale, a conventional type of reformatory. In addition, some Highfields boys get in difficulty again
after they complete the course.

Early in the experiment, Dr. McCorkle decided to try some scientific evaluation of his program. He set up an elaborate, five-year study,
comparing boys who "graduated" from Highfields with those who
left Annandale. The results were astonishing. Although 51 percent
of the boys from Annandale got into trouble again, or recidivated,
only 23 percent of the Highfields boys had further difficulties with
the law.

Almost immediately—as so often happens in the delinquency field—the experts went to work and clobbered the findings. The figures were attacked far and wide. Researchers pointed out that Highfields boys were hand-picked because judges thought they would benefit by the treatment, whereas Annandale had to take on all comers.

In an attempt to meet this criticism, which McCorkle felt had some validity, a second survey was made. The records of a group of Annandale boys were studied in depth—boys who had been committed to the reformatory *before Highfields had opened*. They were chosen because they had exactly the same characteristics and background and degree of delinquency which *would* have landed them in Highfields if such an institution had existed. These boys' records were then compared with the Highfields boys. In the light of this new study, the record was still impressive. Highfields boys who got into trouble again were just about half the number of Annandale boys who backslid. But researchers will tell you Highfields hasn't been "proved."

One of the more attractive features of the Highfields approach is the cost. The average stay is about four months, and the total bill is $650. On the other hand, the average stay at Annandale is roughly a year, and the cost is just over $2,000 (a much lower figure than in most states). Therefore, *even if the Highfields record of recidivism were no better than Annandale's,* it would be preferable for the not-so-serious delinquent because, owing to accelerated treatment, it can do the job for one-third the cost.

No one pretends—and least of all Dr. McCorkle—that the group therapy approach of Highfields is the sole answer for delinquents who reach the courts. It works best on those who have never been institutionalized before and who are not too emotionally disturbed. It also, curiously, has a much higher degree of success among Negroes than whites, although it works well with both groups. But it certainly is one answer for a specific segment of our youngsters who get into trouble. And its ten-year history shows that it works!

The record of Highfields is not unknown to the profession. Two books have been written on the subject, a television program was built around its activities, and many foreign visitors have praised its

methods. The state of New Jersey has been sufficiently impressed to
start two more "Highfields" in other sections—one for boys and one
for girls—with a third one, of an experimental nature, being tried in
Newark to see if the principle will work in a large city where the
boys go home at night instead of sleeping at the institution. In addition, the state of New York, largely on the recommendation of Gov-
ernor Rockefeller's young assistant for juvenile affairs, Alexander
Aldrich, has announced its intention of starting a Highfields-type
center, and the city of Provo, Utah, has a similar enterprise under
way. Even in Scandinavia I found the authorities planning to adopt
certain features of the Highfields plan.

The obvious question to ask, of course, is: Why has an idea which
works so well for ten years in one state, and costs so little to operate,
not been adopted by many of our other states?

The question will come up frequently in this section of the book.
It can perhaps best be answered by Dr. McCorkle's own remark,
quoted earlier, to the effect that the experts "are committed to their
own brand of magic." Frequently, good ideas are not imitated because
they run contrary to the doctrine of the reigning practitioners in the
area. In a field where orthodoxy is rife, new ideas are often heresy.
Some delinquency-fighting systems have been operating successfully
for twenty-five years, and yet no one bothers to adopt them elsewhere.
If the subject is brought up at all, the answer is invariably: "But it
hasn't *really* been proved!" And since just about nothing has "really"
been proved by researchers, at least to the satisfaction of other researchers, the matter is apt to rest there.

When the subject of small institutions is brought up, for example,
just about every penologist in the world agrees that the smaller the
institution, the greater the chance of success. And yet, in the next
sentence, one is apt to be told that in this country at least we can't
afford to have small institutions. They cost too much money. However,
Highfields is a small institution that costs less than a large one.
Nevertheless, almost no one outside of New Jersey has seen fit to
copy it.

In sum then, one can say that, in addition to the group therapy
method as practiced at Highfields, the psychological approach has
validity in fighting delinquency in the following ways:

1. Diagnostics.
2. A general understanding of personal relationships.
3. The treatment of those relatively few delinquents (possibly 10 percent) who are seriously disturbed.

Tapped in a limited way, without committing ourselves to the impossible goal of psychoanalyzing every kid who gets into trouble, this approach can be useful. On the other hand, individual psychiatry is expensive. We might as well face the fact that taxpayers will probably never make sufficient funds available to handle large numbers of delinquents on this basis. And even if such money were forthcoming, there is doubt that this would be the best way to spend it. Other approaches are more effective and less costly.

The trick in treating delinquency is to remember that psychology is only one weapon. It is not an entire arsenal.

9

THE PHYSIOLOGICAL APPROACH

THIS approach views the delinquent not so much in a psychological way as a physical, or biological one. Adherents of this theory feel that most misbehavior of "disturbed youngsters" results from an organic malfunctioning of the body. And the most dramatic example I found of this way of thinking was in Baltimore.

Diane Kent (that is not her real name) is today a strikingly lovely girl of eighteen with fresh skin, blond hair and brown eyes. Popular, vivacious and bright, she's just starting college. She's unofficially engaged to a young Marine flier with whom she's very much in love, and, as far as her classmates can tell, she hasn't a problem in the world.

What her classmates do not know, however, is that she owes her present serenity to drugs, which she may have to remain on for the rest of her life. Furthermore, although she belongs to that middle-class society which so infrequently becomes a juvenile delinquency statistic, Diane has been as "delinquent" as many a girl in an institution. The mother of an illegitimate baby, she has a background of drinking, sexual promiscuity and monumental hell-raising that goes back to the age of thirteen.

The Kents live in a tidy, red-brick house in an attractive, middle-income Baltimore suburb. The father has a good office job; the mother is warm, articulate and intelligent, and has always stayed at home to look after her four children. The family is strongly Catholic.

What Mrs. Kent calls "the family nightmare" began five years ago. Diane, just before starting high school, began to be withdrawn and quiet. She would go into her room for hours, lock the door and play jazz records. She also began picking up with boyfriends that were not of her age and background—older boys who drank a lot and rode around late at night in cars. Her parents talked to her but it seemed to do little good. By the end of her freshman year in high school, she had found a boy of twenty, Nick, whom she brought home. She seemed little interested in the boys and girls in her neighborhood or in her school.

One night, when she was still thirteen, she sneaked out her bedroom window. Late that night, she was picked up by the police with Nick and some other boys in an alley. All of them were drinking beer and appeared intoxicated. The police brought Diane home to her shocked parents, who had thought she was in bed. They learned that Nick had a police record for drinking and stealing. Diane was not booked, and the family forbade her to see Nick or to leave her room at night thereafter.

Not very many nights later, however, a neighbor told Mrs. Kent that she had seen Diane crawling in through her bedroom window at 5 A.M. When the family confronted the girl with this information, she displayed a ring and said she planned to marry Nick. Mrs. Kent reasoned with her in as understanding a way as she could, but she didn't feel she was getting through to the girl. Diane, however, even though she displayed apathy, promised to behave. Several nights later, Mrs. Kent went to Diane's room shortly after she'd retired, and found her gone. A few hours later, the girl crawled back through her bedroom window—with Nick. Mr. Kent called the police, and the boy was taken away, put on probation and warned never to come back.

"By this time, Diane was fourteen, and she was as bad as Nick was," admitted Mrs. Kent. Mr. Kent, for his part, was fed up. The other children were not behaving in this fashion—in fact, they were perfectly normal—and he felt Diane would corrupt all of them. "If she's determined to marry Nick, let her go ahead," he said in disgust. Diane's mother shook her head. "No," she insisted. "She'll be all right."

Somebody told Mrs. Kent about a psychiatrist called Dr. Frank Ayd, and she decided to take Diane to him. "I felt idiotic about calling him," she explained. "I felt that somewhere my discipline with Diane had failed, and that I was to blame, not my daughter. On the other hand, we'd given Diane exactly the same upbringing we'd given the other children, and yet nothing seemed to work with her—reasoning, punishment, coercion."

Dr. Ayd examined Diane and said to Mrs. Kent, "You have a very sick girl." Her brain wave activity was far from normal, according to an electroencephalogram test, and she was suffering from an acute anxiety neurosis. Some people, with similar conditions, will wash their hands excessively or suffer stomach spasms, he explained; Diane picked up boys. He put her on a regime of drugs which he warned would not take effect immediately, and sent her home.

During the next few weeks, she attempted to climb out of her room at night, and when she was restrained by the family, she tried to commit suicide. At this point, Dr. Ayd, feeling a long period of rehabilitation was indicated, put her in a hospital for five months. She seemed to respond to treatment, and she was allowed to come home.

"From that time on, our life entered a new phase of terror," says Mrs. Kent. "She picked up boys on the street. She came home drunk. She went with horrible people. I slept in her room as often as I could so she couldn't get out. We put grates and padlocks on the windows and doors. Then one night she picked the lock, got out and brought a boy home with her. A few months later, she announced she was going to have a baby."

Diane went back to the hospital to have her baby. When she came home (the baby was adopted as soon as it was born), Diane picked up with a married man.

"She chased *him*. He didn't chase her," admitted Mrs. Kent.

By this time, she was sixteen, and the whole family had begun to collapse under the strain. The other children, two younger and one older, were upset and baffled by the explanations their parents gave them. Feeling that religion might solve the problem where medicine had failed, the family took Diane to a Jesuit priest who had had considerable success in dealing with delinquents. He talked with her and shook his head. He admitted he couldn't get through to her. "It's like talking to a stone wall," he said. "I guess I just don't understand girls."

The family was so distraught at this point that Dr. Ayd, knowing that drugs sometimes take many months before the effects begin to show up, suggested that it might be best to put Diane into a Catholic home for delinquent girls. Mr. Kent agreed. Mrs. Kent, thinking of the other children, was almost persuaded. Then she decided against it. "No," she said suddenly, "we must give Diane one last chance."

She talked with Diane, who, as always, was willing, contrite—and weak. She explained that this was indeed her daughter's last chance. If she failed, Diane would disappear into an institution—perhaps forever.

Mrs. Kent backed up this plea with what amounted to 100 percent surveillance. She rearranged her own life, and that of her husband and other children, so that Diane would never be out of her sight. She slept with her, ate with her, sat with her while she studied, and went for walks with her. Meanwhile, Dr. Ayd stepped up the drug treatment, using new ones that had just become available.

Gradually, during the next six months, Diane began to change. Instead of the lackluster, colorless personality she had become, she began to show an interest in things—in her family, in the house, in the usual activities of an adolescent girl. Young people of Diane's age and background were invited to the house, and she seemed to show some interest in them again.

Even school began to intrigue her. She was way behind in her class, but by working hard, going to summer school and taking extra courses, she caught up sufficiently to graduate. The teachers were amazed at the difference in her. Instead of being withdrawn, she volunteered for things.

By the time she entered college, she had met Fred, the Marine flier, and her improvement was so marked that Dr. Ayd was able to reduce her daily intake of drugs by 85 percent. Eventually, he feels it may be possible for her to get along completely without any.

On the other hand, she may have to take some medication always, like a diabetic. In any event, even if she does, she will otherwise lead a perfectly normal life.

Seeing Diane today, a typical, attractive college coed, I found it hard to believe she was once well on the road toward a prison record. "If she had continued going with the boys she was with," says her mother, "I feel sooner or later she would have ended up stealing cars or worse, and been caught. And with the drinking habits she was developing, she could easily have become a dope addict."

Diane's rehabilitation, largely by miracle drugs but aided of course by an intelligent and self-sacrificing family (her illness cost them $5,000 in medical and hospital bills alone), is a vivid example of the growing theory that much delinquency in the world results from organic, or biological, difficulties and that the cure is simply through drugs and other medical means. Dr. Ayd, moreover, may well be the outstanding exponent of this point of view in the United States. A psychiatrist only thirty-nine years old, he has already had a remarkable career in curing all sorts of mental diseases in both children and adults. He has transferred many of Maryland's asylum inmates to general hospitals where they can be treated as ambulatory patients and lead normal lives.

A Roman Catholic and the father of twelve children himself, Dr. Ayd admits that his religion was a factor in persuading him to pursue the particular methods of treatment he has chosen. Strongly opposed to what he calls the "wild spread" of psychoanalysis in this country to a point where now, in his opinion, it has become synonymous with psychiatry, he stands at the opposite end of the therapeutic pole. He believes in curing people by means other than the analytic couch, and he's had some remarkable results to back up his theory.

A few years ago, for example, he came across a young man in a Navy mental hospital who had committed almost every crime a delinquent could commit, short of murder. The young man—we'll call him Bob Miller—had been undergoing intense psychoanalysis in the hospital for some time, and the analyst had come to the conclusion that all the boy's difficulties had been brought about because at an early age his father had made him wear long winter underwear and the youngster was ashamed to undress in the locker room with the other boys. Bob had reached a point of depression where he was afraid and unwilling to leave the hospital.

Dr. Ayd was called in to examine the boy, and decided he could be helped by a new drug called Mebarol. Since the young man responded to this treatment, Dr. Ayd encouraged him to leave the hospital, get a job and go back to school at nights. Eventually, he finished high school, and went on to Loyola College. When he graduated, he got a job teaching. He married, and is now the father of five children. He still has to take Mebarol every morning (his children remind him if he forgets it), but otherwise he leads a normal, useful life. "I had been classified as incurable," he told me. "I believe Dr. Ayd gave me back my life."

Not all treatment is by drugs, of course. Sometimes people require shock treatment, surgery, even lobotomies. Brain damage is frequently present in delinquents, and this shows up only when an electroencephalogram is taken.

Many times, of course, there is an obvious physical defect, easy for all to see. And those wise in the ways of handling delinquents look first for these things, things which could lead a youngster into trouble.

In Boston, a young boy turned to delinquency because he was revolting against the taunts he had heard all his life about his "cock-eyes" (strabismus). When the court turned him over to Boston's Citizenship Training Program as a condition of his probation, the director, Louis Maglio, quickly sized up the situation and arranged for the boy to go to an eye clinic. There a surgeon took on the job of straightening the boy's eyes. Today, the delinquent is leading a normal life as a successful television repair man.

In Philadelphia, the Youth Center had a thirteen-year-old delinquent whose glandular weakness made his body obese and his sex organs abnormally small. For this reason, he hated to take a shower with other boys. In order to prove his manhood, he decided to break into a store. When he was picked up by the police and taken to the Center, the director sent him to an endocrine clinic where he was treated with hormones. Eventually, he developed a normal physique, and never got into trouble again.

Defects of this kind are simple to spot, and people who deal with children have been aware of their importance for years. However, the hidden, mental defects—the kind that can be detected and treated only by the most sophisticated machinery and methods—are much harder to uncover.

For example, in Baltimore not long ago, a sixteen-year-old Negro was about to go on trial for his life. Nicknamed "Lover Boy" by the press, he was accused of murdering his girl friend because, it was said, she would not sleep with him. As things shaped up, it looked as though "Lover Boy" were going to get the works. But in reading about the case in the papers, Dr. Ayd was struck by certain discrepancies in the boy's account of what happened. He decided to see the youngster. He had a long talk with him, during which the boy complained of "blackouts." Dr. Ayd ordered an electroencephalogram taken, and the defendant was found to be an epileptic, although his was the kind which did not produce convulsions. Instead of being put on trial, the boy was transferred to the state hospital.

"Lover Boy," Diane Kent and Bob Miller are all biologically deficient. They exhibit the outward behavior of the usual delinquents, but are driven by physical factors over which they have little control. They appear normal, but do not respond to the normal methods of treatment. Punishment, or cracking down on them, has no effect. It only makes the situation worse. Fortunately, modern instruments can detect such abnormalities, and modern drugs developed in the last few years can treat them.

Freud, the father of psychoanalysis, felt that eventually chemical causes would be found for mental illnesses. And a psychiatrist like Dr. Ayd believes that we have not only found some of the chemical causes but some of the chemical cures. As far as psychoanalysis is concerned, he believes it has given us an important insight into human behavior and that it is interesting as a philosophy, but he is convinced it's "practically useless" as a therapy. "The Freudian analysts," he declares, "really treat symptoms rather than causes." And in pursuing that growing branch of science called "biological psychiatry," he believes that eventually most mental patients will leave our institutions and will lead normal lives, even though, like diabetics, they may have to take some kind of medicine the rest of their lives.

Like all people who become caught up in a new and promising approach, Dr. Ayd may be overenthusiastic about its possibilities. It is my own feeling that he is overenthusiastic in estimating the number of arrested delinquents who have physical disorders and who can be cured by modern medicine in one way or another. In his opinion, the figure is between 70 and 80 percent. (The reader will remember that in the last chapter the psychoanalyst estimated that 100 percent of the delinquents could, and should, be helped by psychoanalysis!)

In any event, no one in this country has made any serious attempt to discover the number of delinquents who would fit into the "biological" category. It is interesting to note that in Tokyo, Japan's largest Classification Center has found that almost 50 percent of its delinquents have some physical disability. It may be considerably less than that in this country, where the standard of living is higher, but certainly the figure is substantial enough to warrant giving careful attention to this method of detection and treatment whenever a delinquent gets into anything more than minor difficulties.

Under the present circumstances, for example, only youngsters with means are able to afford the luxury of having an electroencephalogram taken when they run into trouble. (The cost is between $50 and $75.) Dr. Ayd, for one, believes that *all* court cases of delinquency should automatically be given such tests to determine if the youngster's brain is functioning normally. He believes it should be as automatic as a blood test. If done under court auspices, he is of the opinion that the cost could be reduced about half. If, as a case in point the 450,000 delinquents who went through our courts last year were given such tests, the cost would have been about $13.5 million. Since juvenile delinquency is said to cost the nation $200 million a year, the smaller sum of money would be well spent if it helped us get at the real cause—and in many cases the real cure— for that percentage of our delinquents who are suffering from some kind of biological disorder. The vast majority of our delinquents are tried, sentenced and punished without such tests, and we have no idea how large a part the youngster with such problems plays in our total picture. It would be interesting—and comparatively inexpensive—to find out.

10

THE SOCIOLOGICAL APPROACH

THE social concept of delinquency—perhaps the most popular one of all—holds, in simplest terms, that the youngster is not the victim of inner psychological conflicts or of some biological difficulty, but is rather the victim of his environment. He is the hapless product of the disruptive social forces around him, forces over which he has little or no control.

Our most stylish theories at the moment revolve around this concept. Lower-class subculture, status discontent, inequality of opportunity, slum clearance, recreational facilities, even racial integration can all be lumped in this ideological bin.

Now the trouble with casting doubt on any of these ideas as delinquency dampeners is that the doubter is put in the position of favoring sin rather than virtue. I would like to state firmly that I am not against virtue or even many of the things which sociologists urge upon us. I feel, for example, there should be intelligent slum clearance, adequate housing, good health services, numerous playgrounds and settlement houses, equality of opportunities for jobs and education and, of course, racial integration. With our great wealth, our background of pioneering in many fields, our interest in overseas missionaries, Marshall Plans and Rockefeller Foundation grants, as well as our general history of trying to make the world a better place to live in, these things should have been done a long time ago. But I do question the wisdom of embarking on such programs, not for themselves, but in the fervent belief that they will solve our delinquency problems. With the exception of giving the Negro a chance at first-class citizenship, perhaps none of these things will influence delinquency one way or the other.

As we have seen in the preceding chapters, however, there are some good results in almost all approaches. And in the sociological sphere, perhaps nothing has been more successful—nor, again, so little imitated—as the famous Chicago Area Project.

Founded almost thirty years ago by the late Clifford Shaw and his assistant, Henry D. McKay, the Project was based on the revolutionary idea that *slum people could handle their own children*. Feeling that the trouble with most do-good programs was that they attempted to reform people by the use of outsiders, Shaw attempted to do the job from the inside. He determined to enlist the aid of those living in the community itself—the truck drivers, the schoolteachers, the ministers, the grocers, the ex-convicts, the housewives. He would offer advice and counsel, and occasionally a helper and a little money, as a pump primer. But on the whole the job would be done by the people themselves.

He selected as his first project the Russell Square community on the South Side. It was a Polish section where the character-building services—the Y.M.C.A., the boys clubs, the Sunday schools, etc.— were not reaching the offenders. The neighborhood was ridden with crime, delinquency and gangs.

The first pump primer to enter this blighted section was James F. McDonald, whose sole sociological weapon was a soft ball and a bat. He was probably the first "gang worker" in America, the forerunner of an established profession today. Only twenty-seven years old, he went from alley to alley, mingling with the kids. At first, they refused to play ball with him ("What's your angle, mister?"). They were naturally suspicious, thinking he was a truant officer or a cop in plain clothes, but gradually they lost their fear of him and succumbed. What boy wouldn't? He never preached and he never moralized. But whenever he could, he talked with the adults and encouraged them to form a committee to improve their neighborhood. When they did, one of the first things the committee did was to take over an abandoned parochial school and turn the basement into a clubroom for a boys club.

The clubroom worked out well, and people were encouraged. One thing led to another. Soon the community committee and other interested groups raised $40,000 to rebuild the second floor of the old school into a modern gymnasium. Then someone suggested buying an old portable school building for $25, and moving it to a leased lake-front site as a picnic ground and summer camp. Before long, they raised enough money to buy twenty-six acres of land in Indiana as a permanent camp site. All the work in fixing it up was donated by neighborhood carpenters, plumbers, plasterers and machinists, who did it in their spare time.

In no time at all, this one-time "contemptible neighborhood" had become a respected one in the eyes of the city. Particularly the politicians. They began to sniff the power of an organized community and there's no headier aroma to a politician up for election. They saw to it that garbage was collected daily instead of weekly, that parks were kept up, that streets were cleaned and that police protection was adequate.

But long before all these things had come to pass, McDonald, Shaw, McKay and their associates had moved on to other neighborhoods. They had done their job. They were always available for consultation if needed, but they knew that once a community really got aroused, it generally kept going by virtue of its own momentum.

The Chicago Area Project idea grew until it was taken over by the state of Illinois as part of its Youth Commission. Today, its executive head is Anthony Sorrentino, who operates forty similar projects throughout Chicago and other cities in the state. It has not abolished the delinquency problem, but most people living in the projects feel that it has helped. There has been a general downward trend in delinquency figures in these areas, but because of the many factors involved which could account for it, the sponsors felt it was impossible to make any precise scientific measurement of its success and none has been undertaken.

One of the important by-products of the Area Project is that it has forced people to think hard about the wisdom of superimposing reform ideas from the outside. It has also forced agencies to look at a community as a whole, not just as a single group or a single family, and to organize *all* resources in behalf of neighborhood kids. When everybody's in the act, and the butcher and the baker and the candy store proprietor are on the delinquency subcommittee, the chances of success are heightened. Furthermore, there probably just isn't enough money around to bring in from outside all the things that are needed for kids anyway. The community *must* do most of it for itself.

"You can't just bring in services and expect them to solve a problem," Dr. McKay told me. "They don't get at the basic causes."

The Chicago Area Project idea has its limitations. It operates best in communities that are not in such a state of upheaval or flux that there's nothing to build on. Poverty, slums and crime do not defeat the Project idea. But if people are moving in and out rapidly, and there are no established businesses, churches, clubs or other organizations upon which a community spirit can be built, the idea can fail.

On the whole, however, the Project has been worthwhile, and the idea is one of the more respected in the field. But in spite of this, and in spite of the fact that bits and pieces of the plan have been taken over by other people in other parts of the country, the truth is that the Chicago Area Project has remained pretty much where it started many years ago—in Illinois.

Why?

Like so many effective methods, it ran contrary to the interests of others operating in the field. The latter had their own approaches to the problem. They had sold their backers on an idea, and they didn't want to admit somebody else's was better.

For another thing, its progenitor, Dr. Shaw, didn't have too much respect for "professionals." Although he did not discourage his workers from getting all the degrees they could, he was much more interested in using people with natural aptitudes rather than academic qualifications. Furthermore, with his method of letting the local citizens do the bulk of the work, there was not much need for vast numbers of professionals.

But last and most important, Shaw was not a tub-thumper. He modestly—and mistakenly—believed that promotion was unnecessary if you had a good idea. Perhaps his first street worker, James Mc-

Donald, summed it up best for me recently when he said, "Shaw's idea was valid—to work from the bottom up rather than from the top down. But he believed that if his idea was good, people would adopt it automatically. He didn't believe in spreading his gospel. And in his retiring manner, he invited obscurity. The world did *not* beat a path to his door. A few sociologists knew about the Project, but the country as a whole knew—and still knows—nothing about it."

As we have seen, the best candidate for any community approach to delinquency is one that is settled and homogeneous—be it Polish, Negro, Jewish, Irish, Puerto Rican, etc. Russell Square succeeded because, even though it was a depressed neighborhood—it was, in fact, a Polish ghetto, if by "ghetto" we mean a low-income area where people of predominantly one nationality or religion live—all the stable elements of an established community were there to build on.

In a settled all-Negro community, for example (and New York's Harlem is *not* one since it is largely infiltrated with Puerto Ricans), delinquency is less than in a community that is shifting its base. In Baltimore, Bernard Lander, studying Negro and white neighborhoods, found that delinquency rates were highest in areas of maximum racial mixing. In Honolulu, it has been shown that when the Japanese lived in a well-knit racial ghetto, delinquency was far less than when they mixed in with the rest of the population. And in New York City's Chinatown, where eight thousand Chinese are crowded into a poor neighborhood, juvenile delinquency is virtually non-existent.

"We don't mind ghettoization," a well-to-do Chinese who could afford to live elsewhere told me there. "We like to be left alone. We have our community centers, our family societies, our traditions. We prefer it this way."

The idea of a ghetto, of course, is repugnant to the American mentality. And most Americans hope that the day will soon come when people of all races can live side by side in any community they choose. For ghettoization, however cozy it may be as far as controlling delinquency is concerned, is certainly not the wave of the future, any more than the Japanese feudal system or Turkish tribal setup are. Consequently, when our Negro, Jewish, Irish or Puerto Rican communities break up, as they do sooner or later (even Chinatown, the model ghetto, is dispersing), we must be prepared for trouble and have measures ready that will counteract it.

As the Negroes break out of their traditional mold, for example, things could be done to cushion the shock. For one thing, a sound housing policy. When slums are cleared, our absurd low-cost housing regulations tend to exaggerate, rather than cushion, the shock. The results can be disastrous. Ben Conte, one of New York City's gang worker supervisors who works nightly in a new housing development, summed up his feelings in these words: "As far as kids are concerned, the old houses were far better than the new ones!"

Harrison Salisbury, in *The Shook-Up Generation,* called the Fort Greene housing project in Brooklyn, which is the largest in the world, a "$20,000,000 slum." Because of improper planning, because of a lack of conditioning the new occupants for the changeover, the project residents ironically look back with longing at the old, broken-down hovels they used to live in. There, at least, they knew everybody, the neighborhood had a personality, and there was not the crushing anonymity, loneliness and ugliness of high-rise apartments.

"It's just like a fortress," a Negro mother in Jersey City's new Booker T. Washington Houses told me. "You don't know your neighbors. In building this development, they just built a building. They didn't build any of the activities we had in the old place—the neighborhood stores, the friends, the parks and all the rest."

The outstanding evil of low-cost housing, of course, is the low-income ceiling. As soon as a tenant reaches it, out he must go. The ones who remain behind are largely the dispossessed, the failures, the welfare cases. The result is ghettoization of the most depressing kind because the children do not have a chance to meet and mingle with, and be inspired by, successful people.

"The able, rising families are constantly driven out as their incomes cross the ceiling figures," says Mr. Salisbury. "By screening applicants for low-rent apartments to eliminate those with even modest wages, the new community is badly handicapped. It is deprived of the normal quota of human talents needed for self-organization, self-discipline and self-improvement. A human catchpool is formed that breeds social ills and requires endless outside assistance."

Ray Brown, head of Jersey City's National Association for the

Advancement of Colored People, put it similarly. "Where," he asked me, "are you going to get leadership when you drain off all those who are successful? It is small wonder that when a new housing project opens, there is an invariable rise in delinquency."

Aside from better planning and a revision of income ceilings, another way to cushion the shock when Negroes and others go into new housing developments is to provide some sort of gainful activities for the young just out of school. One day, I sat in the Booker T. Washington Houses and talked with an endless stream of Negro youngsters, between fifteen and eighteen, who had spent days looking for full or part-time jobs without success. There was simply nothing for those to do who lived in apartments and were not interested in school. At a period when kids are thirsting for excitement, they just sit around or walk around looking for something to do, preferably something with a touch of adventure. This situation is naturally eyed uneasily by the police, and although Jersey City is 25 percent Negro, I found the police were universally accused by housing project tenants of being anti-Negro. In two apartments, for example, I found seven Negro boys, all of whom had been picked up by the police on nonspecific charges. Another boy, Dan, fifteen, admitted he had stolen a car. He said he had been beaten all night by rubber hoses by the police and finally hit in the head with a gun butt. Still another boy, Phil, sixteen, said that whenever he walked more than a block or two away from the housing project, he was apt to be picked up by "the man" (the police) just for being away from his home. It is not surprising that some of our biggest cities are worried about what they call a rising tide of hostility toward policemen, especially by Negroes.

Whether the latter are more prone to be picked up by the police or not will, of course, be argued by some. However, the fact that Negroes produce crime statistics out of all proportion to their population is not open to question.

Although Negro leaders oppose any over-all breakdown of crime figures by race in the mistaken belief that their people will be unfairly criticized (it seems to me it would be far better if the public realized the magnitude of the problem as a first step in doing something about it), we can get some idea of the situation by looking at the number of Negro youngsters in reformatories and training schools. The ratio of black to white in the general population is about 11 to 89 percent, and yet the ratio in our youth correctional institutions is 33 to 67 percent, or about three times the population percentage. The *Journal of Negro Education* estimates that, for the country as a whole, Negroes contribute to the delinquency statistics about twice what they should in proportion to their population. My own feeling is that this figure is low.

Certainly Negroes are discriminated against in jobs and by unions. There are, for example, few Negroes in the Teamsters Union, whose members average between $7,500 and $10,000 a year. The building trades and the service trades also discriminate against Negroes, as do many employers. In many colleges, Negroes find it harder to get scholarships than whites do.

It is interesting to note, at this juncture, that at the turn of the century quite similar discrimination was practiced against the Irish. And gangs at that time were largely made up of Irish hoodlums who swelled the crime statistics. With many avenues of advancement closed to them, the Irish decided to organize and go into politics. Using this as a power wedge, they created a new and improved position for themselves. And as their fortunes rose, there was a corresponding drop in their share in the delinquency figures. The Negroes hope to use the same methods with similar success.

In the meantime, however, many Negro youths—without jobs, without much interest in our type of high school, without the status that comes with money in the pocket, without a friendly police, without much to do in the "fortress" setting of a new housing development, and without much possibility of satisfying an adolescent's acute longing to play a part in adult society—quite naturally form clubs or gangs, and practice togetherness with zip guns.

The youngsters themselves call such organizations "clubs." The rest of the world calls them gangs, especially if they are hostile. Many gangs, of course, both Negro and white, are purely social, harmless and seem to satisfy a kid's instinct to participate in this aspect of the tribal rites of childhood. This latter kind we will not consider here. They do not occupy the headlines nor concern the people who are interested in the problem of delinquency.

At the moment, however, our concern is conflict gangs. Most large cities have them, although the police will not admit it in all of them. New York City, as might be expected, has the largest number—between 120 and 160—involving some eight thousand kids out of a total juvenile population of one and a half million. It possesses perhaps half of all the gangs in the United States.

Although there is nothing new about warring gangs or bands of young hoodlums, there is, fortunately, something new in the way we have learned to cope with them. Spurred on since World War II by highly publicized rumbles and gang killings, our cities have turned more and more to the technique pioneered by James McDonald back in Chicago's Russell Square in the thirties when he was a gang infiltrator for the Area Project.

The method is simple enough. A youngish man, usually between twenty-three and thirty-five, goes to the section of the city where he knows a troublesome gang is operating. He attempts to get to know the members, win their confidence, and eventually channel their hostile and illegitimate activities into peaceful and worthwhile pursuits. If he can, he eventually turns them over to a settlement house or recreation center, and then moves on to other gangs.

All this, of course, takes time and special talent. The worker sometimes has to hang around candy stores or poolrooms for months before he contacts, and wins the friendship of, gang members. Most of the latter are hostile and suspicious, and inclined to look upon the worker as some sort of stool pigeon.

When he does get to know them, he tries to exert the influence that a father or big brother might. He takes them on trips, gives them cigarettes, buys them Cokes, helps their families and tries to get them jobs. He listens to their problems and talks to their probation officers. If there's a real psychotic among them, he gets him help, although this is rarely the case. In general, he tries to keep them out of trouble until maturity takes over.

It is not an easy job. Hours are long—a worker is on call seven days a week and often works into the small hours of the morning—and the pay is small (between $4,000 and $5,000 a year). One has to have dedication to stick with it.

Let us look, for a moment, at one of these workers. Gene Christian is a personable young man of thirty-one, unmarried, who has an itch to be of service in the world. He likes kids and has been working for New York City's Youth Board for three or four years. He doesn't think he's typical because he can't remain detached enough, supposedly a qualification for the job. "You're not supposed to get emotionally involved in a kid's problems," he told me, "but I can't help it. That's the way I am."

His present assignment is in the Washington Heights section of Manhattan. He was sent there shortly after the notorious murder of Michael Farmer, a fifteen-year-old polio cripple who was the victim of a war between the Egyptian Kings, the Dragons and the Jesters over who could use a local swimming pool.

I met Gene in the small office the Youth Board maintains in the area. We talked about his work. When he took on the job, he admits he was "naïve and dewy-eyed."

"A social worker dreams that soon after he arrives on the scene, there will be no more bopping [fighting], no more drinking, no more dope, no more sex orgies," said Gene. "Then comes the disillusionment. You realize these things are not so easy to control as you thought. Gradually, however, you get the feeling that if you can save *one* person, then the whole thing is worthwhile. And when you do finally manage to touch the life of one kid, then you're sure of it."

On this point, the Youth Board agrees with Gene. In New York, it takes at least $3,000 to keep a boy in an institution for a year. If the worker can keep just one boy out, he has justified most of his salary. If he can keep two boys out, the Youth Board—and the state—is ahead of the game.

Gene was initiated into his job dramatically. After hanging around on a street corner talking to some of the kids for a while, one of them suggested they all go for a ride in Gene's old car. He agreed. They got in, and as he turned the ignition key and stepped on the starter, there was a muffled explosion, followed by a puff of smoke. Everybody laughed—except Gene. One of the kids had planted a smoke bomb and wired it to an ignition point. After this disconcerting start, Gene got on well with the kids.

He has learned to take things in his stride. It is not unusual, for example, for him to be awakened at three in the morning because one of his kids has been picked up with a weapon on him. He must get up and go down to the station house to try to straighten out the situation.

Another young worker in the area, Ed Penn, a former Episcopalian priest, has had the satisfaction of seeing the number of boys on probation in his gang go down from fifteen to one during the last year and a half. It has compensated him for the uneasy moments he had when he first took on his job. He was introduced to *his* gang in a park. The first words of greeting were hurled at him from a big seventeen-year-old in the group. "Say, mister, has a Youth Board worker ever been beat up?" he asked.

"I don't think so," said Ed.

"Wanna make history?" asked the other.

While Ed was thinking of a suitable reply to that one, another boy yelled: "Aw, come on! Let's be hospitable!"

Although gang workers are casual and unobtrusive, their actual impact has been considerable, in the opinion of New York's administration. The Youth Board now has more than one hundred workers scattered throughout the city.

"At the moment, we find these workers are the best way to cope with gangs," says Arthur J. Rogers, deputy commissioner of the Board. "Sixty-five fighting gangs have been eliminated since we started, and the large-scale rumble is a thing of the past. We occasionally have a tragic incident, but on the whole gang activity is down. Delinquency, too, shows signs of leveling off in the city."

One of the reasons gang workers are so effective is that they play the role of informers, although no one likes to admit this. As a kind of benign fifth column among the gang members, the worker is in a position to have advance knowledge of rumbles and other activities, and he tips off the police, who stop the thing. Gang kids know this, of course, and it suits them fine. In fact, the success of the whole technique is based on the fact that kids don't really want to fight and are looking for a way of getting out of it without losing face.

"The worker introduces a safety factor into gang conflict because the boys know he will go to great lengths to prevent intergang warfare," says Richard Boone, who operates a successful gang worker program in Chicago under the auspices of the Y.M.C.A. "The worker can always be informed surreptitiously so that police can be called in to prevent a rumble at the last moment if negotiations fail. This enables the gang to assume a tough posture without much risk of really dangerous conflict."

Most gang conflict is based on misunderstanding—misunderstandings about turf (territories), girls and other rights. The gang worker is in a position to mediate these disputes, and they can generally be worked out satisfactorily if people negotiate.

Another reason the worker technique succeeds is that it brings another point of view to a group of kids, and gives them new things to think about. Instead of wanting to have the scrappiest reputation in town, they acquire other goals. They want their gang to be the best dressed, or give the most sought-after dances or have the most successful teams. For example, one of the worst gangs in Philadelphia a few years ago was the Twentieth Century Club. Almost every member had been arrested and done time in institutions. After two years with a gang worker (Philadelphia now has twenty-three of them), the group underwent a reorientation. They changed their name to the Esquires and became a model club, performing numerous community services. One member went on to college. Another opened a successful haberdashery store.

In Chicago, a gang of thirteen boys had one of the most troublesome reputations in town. They broke school windows, stole cars, destroyed property and were branded in school as "a bunch of hoodlums." The local recreation center barred them from its clubrooms. When a young worker was assigned to them, however, a man with considerable athletic ability, he soon had them directed toward more wholesome goals. He played games with them, took them to sports events, and even got them interested in going to church. In fact, the importance the worker assumed in one youngster's life was illustrated by the fact that when the boy was invited by his church to bring his father to a father-son supper, he invited the gang worker rather than his own parent!

The "father image" that the gang worker offers is perhaps crucial to the success of the operation, since most delinquents have unsatisfactory father relationships. Fred D. Hubbard, for example, a young, lanky Negro worker in Chicago with whom I spent considerable time, has had outstanding success because, in a racial group where the matriarchy is the established rule, he has provided his boys with the kind of father substitute that is needed. One of his typical boys, whom I'll call Chuck, was the product of just such a family setup. Chuck was a leader of a gang called the Cobras in the Maxwell Street area. He had been frequently involved with the police and had spent six months in jail as a result of a long delinquent career. Hubbard worked on Chuck until he got him to the point of wanting to lead a more conventional life. Eventually, the gang worker managed to get him a job at Sears Roebuck, where he has done well.

"Today," says Hubbard, "Chuck is married. He has a child. He has bills. He's very much concerned with Sears' profit-sharing plan. He's become a real middle-class type. I'm proud of him!"

As might be expected, the technique of "cooling" gang activity through the infiltration approach has been opposed bitterly. The charges are mainly:

1. It gives undue status to "a bunch of punks."

2. It encourages a gang to act up so that they will have the prestige of being assigned a worker.

3. It is generally ineffectual.

Many police and judges are opposed because they feel it "coddles" kids, and that the gang worker is apt to side with the youngster rather than with the law. Judge Jacob Panken, of New York's Children's Court, wrote not long ago in the *Reader's Digest:*

> Some juvenile authorities, including the New York City Youth Board, insist that the way to deal with these gangs is to "infiltrate" them with social workers who endeavor, by subtle suggestion, to redirect their activities from within. Not only is this method costly and uncertain, but it also gives recognition and status to the gang and the lawless acts on which it is built.

Equally critical of the system is Joseph D. Lohman, Chicago's dynamic sociologist who was once sheriff of Cook County. "Where is the detached [gang] worker who can be a father image to one hundred boys?" he asked me. "Who can give enough of himself to transform the life of a boy?"

Almost immediately afterward, I had the opportunity of putting Lohman's question to Fred Hubbard.

"How can one man have any impact on so many kids?" he repeated rhetorically. "Why, simply by knowing the key men! The impetus for most gang activity filters down from the top. I can stop any rumble in any neighborhood I've been in. If I know there's going to be a riot or a gang fight, I simply get in touch with Chuck or Pete or Sam, and get *them* to stop it. They respect me because they've never had anyone else in their life who's meant anything to them."

For better or worse, most of our large cities with gang problems are committed to the worker approach. In New York City, the mayor's Juvenile Delinquency Evaluation Project issued a report in which it admitted force could not break the terror of teen gangs there. "The break-'em-up-by-force approach fails to come to grips with the real problems and at best merely postpones crime and violence, rather than eliminating them," it said. It recommended the infiltration or gang worker technique, a basis on which the city has been operating since 1948.

Dr. James Short, of the University of Chicago, feels that seventy-five workers can readily control this type of warfare in a city as big as Chicago because they know hours, sometimes days, ahead when trouble will take place. "Indeed, we can say with a big degree of confidence that gang fighting has been eliminated on the part of gangs with which we have worked intensively," he said.

Gangs, of course, are only a small part of the delinquency problem, although their tendency to hit the headlines, the movies and the musical stage makes this hard to realize. In all, there are perhaps fifteen thousand youngsters in the entire country engaged in conflict gang activity, and these are concentrated in our largest cities. For this small but obstreperous fraction of our delinquents, there seems little doubt that gang workers—from the time of James McDonald on—have been successful in their limited way.

Their very success, of course, poses another problem. What do you do with these warring youngsters when you cool them down—woo them away from illegitimate activities and sell them on the advantages of the conventional way of life?

"The street club worker can bring a boy to the point of wanting to lead a different kind of life, of wanting a job, of wanting to dress well and all the rest," says Dr. Short. "But he may also be a kid who's illiterate, who has no concept of steady work, who has no interest in school and no decent place to live. What do you do then? There's no difficulty in stopping gang conflict, but you've got to give kids something to do when you lure them away from the street corners."

There is no doubt that there is a gap between what many kids want and what they can attain. For perhaps the third of our juvenile population *who do not have any interest in college or indeed in school,* there is little to do between sixteen and eighteen. In short, although we tell such boys that by deferring adulthood we are really giving them a greater opportunity in this land of ours, we are in fact doing just the opposite. We are putting such young men (and gang members are usually rational, practical and energetic) in a kind of adolescent deep freeze, and asking them to hold off on everything—job, money, sex, status and, in general, the one thing they want most: the chance to take their place in adult society.

One of the helpful things about organizing a total community in the way the Chicago Area Project does is that, by involving everybody in the problem, rather than the experts, the difficulty is seen as a whole, not just as the business of breaking up a gang. And by seeing the problem as a whole, there is a greater chance to get at the basic causes. Activities and facilities are organized by the community, jobs are dug up and general living conditions are made more agreeable.

Communities, of course, even when they're organized, can do only so much, especially when they are up against basic institutions whose setup often acts as a stumbling block, rather than an aid, in helping kids grow up. And one of these basic institutions is our school system.

11

ARE SCHOOLS DOING THEIR PART?

DR. NEGLEY TEETERS, the fire-eating criminologist of Temple University, was in an incendiary mood when I went to see him.

"I didn't want this interview, you know," he said, when I entered his office. "I've nothing against you, mind, but people write so much and so little is done. I don't think we're getting anywhere with Senate investigations and conferences and headlines. I'm so sick of hearing that the broken home is the cause of delinquency, or the motion picture, or our speeded-up life. The fact is we've *got* to live with our culture. And if you ask me, the crux of our delinquency is not the parents; it's the schools. Our schools are filled with misfits, kids who don't belong. Our education is geared for *all* our kids and that's the heart of the problem. We need some kind of program for the kids who *don't* fit into our school picture, who are *not* interested in middle-class norms or in becoming a lawyer someday."

Dr. Teeters was expressing a point of view which more and more people have come to hold, namely, that our schools are not doing their job. As Dr. William Kvaraceus, of Boston University, has put it: "Our schools face the imminent danger of becoming the most expensive irrelevancy of the twentieth century."

Consider a typical delinquent youngster we'll call John Morris. . . .

John is fifteen. He has a slightly lower-than-average I.Q., and his school grade is a year lower than his age would indicate. His report cards have shown a long list of failures, and he's never really learned to read properly. All his teachers have been women, and he has somehow got the impression that reading, writing and spelling are feminine accomplishments. His family, which is in middle-class circumstances, has moved frequently because his father, working for a large company, has been shifted around. Since John has never been able to understand properly what he's been called upon to study, school to him is pure drudgery, boredom and, worse, humiliation. In the past year or two, finding the situation intolerable, he has played truant more and more. Once he got into trouble for breaking into a store, and he was put on probation. Although he likes to work with his hands and would have made a good gardener, or perhaps a bricklayer, his parents feel this is not in keeping with their status aspirations. Besides, he can't leave school until he's sixteen anyway. Consequently, John sits out the extra year, unhappy, sullen and building up habits of idleness and mischief. He's a headache to the school, and the school is a headache to him.

Now let's look at what might have happened to John if he'd been an Austrian or a Dane or a German.

First of all, he would not have attained his present grade without a good working knowledge of reading and writing, even if he had had to go to school six days a week to do it. Furthermore, the chances are that along the way he would have been exposed to many male teachers and would definitely not have gotten the notion that literacy is largely a female accomplishment. At the age of fourteen, since he did not plan to follow an academic career, he would have been allowed to leave school with the proviso that he enter into an apprenticeship as a stonemason or a gardener or a forester or some other trade. Under this arrangement, he would have had from four to seven years of on-the-job training with a first-rate master. During this time, he would also have had to go to a trade school one day a week.

The U.S. answer to the European approach is the vocational high school. This exists in many large cities, but on the whole it is for boys and girls with fairly good academic qualifications. There are some exceptions. A few—very few—of our big cities have trade programs which take youngsters of lower-than-average ability and attempt to instruct them in paperhanging or upholstering or needlework. But such programs touch the merest fraction of our high school enrollment. Speaking for the country at large, there is little place in our system for the boy or girl with few or no academic qualifications, for the child, as some people put it bluntly, who would make a good second-class citizen.

In accordance with the American dream, everybody must want to be, and be able to be, a first-class citizen. Anything less is un-American. Consequently, a largely uniform school system has been geared to this ideal. It is book-centered and college-oriented, which is fine for those going on to higher education. But it leaves no alternatives for a fellow like John.

The results of this rigid approach are crushing. Almost one million youngsters a year drop out of high school. Many just sweat it out, doing little or nothing, until the legal age of leaving (sixteen in some states, seventeen in others). Some are embittered, frustrated and, worse, functionally illiterate. In the name of democracy and with high humanitarian purpose, we have short-changed a large segment of our juvenile population and not given them the kind of education *which would have been right for them.*

Realizing that something was wrong and unable to lower the legal age at which kids might leave school, the education authorities have tried to fill the gap with substitutes—counselors, psychologists, playgrounds, "practical" courses and extracurricular activities. Some of these have been helpful, but they have not got to the heart of the problem. Counselors are worthwhile, for example, but there are only eleven thousand counselors for nine million high school students. One can see how little individual help can be given, especially when there are no adequate educational alternatives for the counselors to recommend anyway.

Dr. Kvaraceus estimates that only about 35 percent of our youth have the ability to profit from a traditional college-prepartory curriculum, and that the academically untalented youngster, the "reluctant learner" as some educators like to call him, is unprovided for. This point of view was confirmed by a recent National Education Association study of the teachers themselves. After listing "overlarge classes" as their number one problem, the teachers designated "the reluctant learner" as problem number two. Forty-five percent of the teachers urged that some provision be made outside the regular classroom for nonlearners, and almost half the principals endorsed this suggestion. Moreover, the Conant report subtly urged that these youngsters might be eased out of school at fourteen, if they couldn't, or wouldn't, learn.

It might be interesting at this point to take a look at the I.Q. distribution of the nation's children as a whole.

They run roughly as follows:

2.5% I.Q. lower than 70	25% I.Q. 70-90	45% I.Q. 90-110	25% I.Q. 110-130	2.5% I.Q. higher than 130

The first two sectors, comprising 27.5 percent of our juvenile population, is the segment of our youth that is most handicapped under our educational system. These youngsters are being pushed through the same system as everybody else, in the illusion that such things are more democratic.

Far from being democratic, this situation is highly undemocratic in that it denies to a large group of youngsters a training which is geared *for them*. This might be faced with some complacency were it not for the fact that from this "nonlearning" group we draw a good deal of our juvenile delinquency, especially the kind which becomes statistical.

According to judges who handle delinquency cases, a large percentage of the youngsters involved are unable to read. One of New York's children's courts reported that 75 percent of its delinquents had difficulty reading, and that "there is a definite link between reading retardation and delinquency." Street workers have found many gang members unable to read at all, and some have been reported who couldn't ride the subways because they couldn't understand the signs.

In the Gluecks' study of five hundred delinquents matched with five hundred nondelinquents of the same basic intelligence, age, size and background, it was found that while the former were filled with the "spirit of adventure," they were not at all filled with an equal interest in school. In fact, they were a full year behind the nondelinquents in their grades. Moreover, a recent Ford Foundation report found that the incidence of delinquency is much higher among the nation's dropouts than among those who continue on through high school. It would seem fairly obvious, therefore, that a very large segment of our youth are not in tune with our educational setup, and because of this, are getting into trouble.

Consequently, it seems to me there are two possible solutions:

1. Such youngsters can leave school earlier.

2. If they are required to stay until present age limits, schools can provide educational alternatives to them, things which will interest the so-called "nonlearner" who can make a good gardener, cook, nursemaid or maintenance man, but is not a potential lawyer, schoolteacher or business executive.

"What perversion of democracy makes us feel that everybody must *want* to be a general, never a sergeant?" a school principal once asked me.

In other parts of the world this problem is often approached more realistically. In Thailand, for example, which devotes a far larger share of its national budget to education than we do (30 percent), education is compulsory only to the age of fourteen. However, schools, colleges and universities are free to all, and those interested in an academic career can go on to higher learning if they want to and if they are capable of it.

As we have seen in Germany and Austria, a boy or girl not interested in books can leave school at fourteen, but he is not just thrown on the street corner. Alternatives have been set up, generally of an apprenticeship nature. In France, where one can leave school at fifteen, there is a similar setup. Denmark also has a fourteen-year-old limit for school, *but those who leave must definitely be embarked on other careers.* England had a school limit of fourteen years until recently, when it raised the age to fifteen. It is interesting that when this happened, the peak of juvenile delinquency suddenly rose from fourteen to fifteen. It is equally interesting to note that in Sweden, which has a very high delinquency quotient, the legal age at which one can leave school is sixteen—*the same as ours!*

These experiences would seem to indicate that leaving school earlier—at least leaving the *conventional* type of school—tends to curb delinquency. But on the other hand, such implications do not mean that formal education must be stopped. They simply mean that *different kinds* of learning must be arranged, within the school system if we wish.

During the past decade a concerted campaign has been waged to curb dropouts and try to get everyone through our high schools. It has largely failed. Some improvement was noted in the first few years of the campaign, but now the number has leveled off, suggesting that under our present curriculum probably very few more youngsters can be induced to stay.

Says Dr. Kvaraceus: "Indications are that the holding power of the public schools, presently graduating sixty out of a hundred persons, seventeen years of age, has probably reached its peak. Unless the curriculum is broadened . . . universal secondary education will remain an American myth."

Although very few alternatives to the present curriculum have been created, and although we have more or less insisted that everybody conform to a uniform approach, here and there a breakthrough has occurred—a glimpse of what could be done. This has not been accomplished, though, without strong opposition.

Several of the most interesting breakthroughs, for example, have occurred in the Philadelphia area. Since 1943, the school system there has had a work-study program operating whereby youngsters can work part time and study part time. Similar programs, designed to discourage dropouts, have been operating in Rochester, New York, Santa Barbara, California, and other cities. In Philadelphia at the moment, about two thousand out of a total enrollment of 240,000 school children are engaged in such a program, a figure representing less than one percent of the total. And unfortunately the program has been declining in recent months because of the drying-up of job opportunities for youngsters.

In an attempt to do something about the job situation for young, potentially delinquent pupils, the city recently decided to go into action on an experimental basis, with the cooperation of school officials and labor unions. In effect, a municipal adaptation of the Civilian Conservation Corps was created. It is called, appropriately, the Youth Conservation Corps.

It works as follows:

Boys between the ages of fourteen and seventeen who are having trouble in school, and often with the police as well, are enrolled in the Corps, which is operated by the Department of Public Welfare. When school is in session, the boys go to classes only in the morning. At noon they are dismissed, picked up by buses, given a lunch and working clothes in a central office, and transported to a city park where they spend the rest of the day raking, clearing brush, digging drain ditches and doing other park improvement projects. On Saturdays, they put in a full day of work in the parks, and during the summer they work full time. The boys are paid from thirty to sixty cents per hour, depending on the quality of their work.

From the beginning, the program, which involves four hundred boys and has been operating several years, ran into opposition. Most of it came from the park workers' union. William J. McEntee, president of the American Federation of State, County, and Municipal Employees local district council, who was in favor of the idea, said that it took about three months to convince the union concerned that the project would not take any jobs away from regular workers, and would be a supplement, rather than a substitute, for their work. "We had a devil of a battle," he admits. Eventually, however, the pilot program got the necessary approval, and the city set aside $200,000 for the experiment.

As things began to roll, it was obvious that the project was going to be a success. The kids worked hard, the parks looked better, and truancy—and delinquency—began to drop. In fact, things worked so well that everybody began taking credit for the idea.

The youngsters themselves showed an enthusiasm that amazed

Deputy Commissioner Clement Doyle, in charge of the project. "They've worked so hard at ordinary park work that it makes you wonder what kind of a job could be done if these kids, who mostly hate school, worked at tasks that really interest them," he said.

Part of the incentive, of course, has been the pay. In winter, boys can earn up to $12 for a twenty-hour week. In summer, they earn up to $24 for a forty-hour week.

"Some kids have come into the Corps with fantastic hair-dos and even stranger clothes," Doyle told me. "But within six months, they are dressing decently and conservatively—with a bit of nudging from their supervisor, of course. Even their speech undergoes a change for the better. And there are few laggards. One boy missed the bus one morning for work, and walked six miles to the park so that he wouldn't miss a day."

Al Williams, a tall, lanky Negro who supervises forty-seven boys, has had the satisfaction of watching youngsters who were problems at school turn into well-behaved kids. "When you know in the morning you're going to spend your afternoons out of doors doing something different and getting paid for it, classes don't seem so boring," he said.

One white boy, Joe, who is fifteen and is in Williams' group, had been a constant truant at Germantown High School. Worse than that, he'd smashed some school windows with a BB gun and gotten into trouble with the authorities. He was recommended by his principal for the Corps last summer. Although Joe was awkward in using tools at first, he developed a fondness for Williams and eventually turned into a good worker. When he returned to school, the principal called up the Negro supervisor. "What have you done to this boy?" he asked. "He's got religion. He no longer plays hooky and he doesn't break windows."

Another boy, a Negro of sixteen and a gang member, had been declared "uneducable" by the school at twelve. By fifteen, he was on probation. He was dirty, clumsy and badly dressed. When he got in the Corps, he tried to play the role of a clown. Unusually slow-moving, he liked to be called "Lightning." Eventually, however, he began to change. He got a haircut for one thing. Then he bought some clothes which he took pride in. Finally one day he said to the other boys: "Don't call me 'Lightning'! Call me by my right name!"

When he finished his course in the Corps (members are limited to six months), he got a certificate of which he is extremely proud. Even better, Williams was able to get him a job as a dishwasher at a luncheonette. Recently, he moved up from dishwasher to assistant chef and tells his ex-Corpsmates, when they go in to see him, that he's "really made it." His supervisor feels he would never have made it in the usual vocational school.

Williams wishes the Corps's six-months rule could be changed. When the time is up, many a boy comes up to him and says, "What am I going to do? I don't want to go back to school. That's the reason I came into the Corps." Williams considers the time limit a big disadvantage.

Another disadvantage, of course, is that park work has its limits. After the first year of operation, it was apparent that other work would have to be found for the boys during those winter days when outdoor work was impossible. Since the subways were dirty and since the city did not have enough regular employees to clean them, it was decided the boys could be put to work washing down the walls. Subway maintenance men fought the idea at first, but were gradually convinced that the boys were not going to take away any of their jobs. And when the youngsters finally went to work, the maintenance men were surprised at the speed with which the boys accomplished the job. Philadelphians, moreover, on their way to and from work, were pleased to see dirty, dingy subway walls clean for the first time in their memories.

All of the boys engaged in the Corps project have been poor students academically. As a result, their attendance and conduct records at school were also poor. When they joined the Corps, however, the youngsters' relationship with the schools took a turn for the better. Teachers stopped complaining about their misbehavior, and truancy dropped as well. Many of the boys even began getting better grades, as their attitude toward study changed.

In 1960, a study was made to determine the effectiveness of the program as far as delinquency was concerned. Out of 113 boys studied, 60 of them (more than half) had had police contacts during the previous summer. One year later, however, these same boys, now enrolled in the Corps, produced only seven police contacts. *The arrest figure had dropped from 53 to 6 percent!*

As far as cost is concerned, the city so far has paid out $447 per youngster. It has, of course, received some return in the form of municipal improvements. Even more important, it has saved the cost of arresting, adjudicating and institutionalizing young criminals.

Philadelphia's Youth Corps program is unique. It is also limited. Although it points the way, it is only a tentative gesture in the direction of delinquency prevention. To be truly effective with "non-learners," the program's base must be broadened considerably so that not only leaf-raking and wall-washing are brought into it, but all sorts of other occupations as well. This will, of course, call for much more cooperation on the part of labor, management, taxpayers and local governments than now exists. Nevertheless, the Philadelphia program has been a start. And it has been sufficiently effective for the U.S. Department of Health, Education, and Welfare to urge other cities to adopt similar programs. In a speech citing the "dramatic reduction in police contacts among boys active in the Corps" as well as "marked adjustment in school difficulties," Philip G. Green, Health, Education, and Welfare's division director, called on every big city to copy the idea.

Aside from helping to make possible such job alternatives for the academically disinclined, Philadelphia's school system has taken the lead in establishing a Case Review Committee which meets once a week and decides what to do about public school children who are potentially dangerous to themselves or to others.

The committee was established twelve years ago as a result of a scandal that panicked the City of Brotherly Love into the need for doing something about its problem children. A sixteen-year-old boy of good family murdered a fourteen-year-old under especially grim circumstances. The older boy met the younger one for the first time in a movie theater and invited him to his home on the pretext of seeing his chemistry set. The older boy made sexual advances to his new friend. When he was rebuffed, he stabbed him thirty times and then trussed him up behind the garage.

Since that time, the resultant committee has met weekly to consider cases that are submitted to them by teachers and principals—

children who are special problems. This attempt at preventing delinquency before it gets started handles roughly a hundred cases a year, cases that might have resulted in tragedies like the preceding one if not caught in time. Potential murderers, arsonists and rapists have been uncovered in this way, and steps have been taken to render them harmless. Sometimes a psychiatrist was necessary, sometimes a new home, sometimes counseling, and occasionally—very occasionally—an institution. More often than not, however, nothing was needed except some "home work" with the parents.

In carrying out Case Committee assignments and other problems, the Philadelphia school system has a corps of full-time counselors, psychologists, psychiatrists and attendance officers whose 430 members form a department called Pupil Personnel and Counseling. Headed by able Robert C. Taber, this department is one of the largest social service units in the city. Its growth over the last few years is a reflection of the feeling that schools can do much more than they have been doing in preventing delinquency, especially since teachers see more of children every day than anybody else except parents.

"Schools are in a unique position to identify maladjustment early in the lives of children and to differentiate between 'growing pains' and the beginnings of a deep-seated emotional disturbance," says Taber.

He also believes that flexibility and a willingness to try new ideas is one of the most important assets a school system can have. And just as Philadelphia school officials have not hesitated to try out the idea of a Case Review Committee, of work-study programs, or of giving pupils credits for work in the municipal Youth Conservation Corps, they have also turned up an interesting approach to the problem of high school girls with illegitimate babies.

A study of unwed mothers ten years ago revealed that less than 10 percent of the girls returned to school. Furthermore, many of them, because of a lack of supervision or of any compelling interests, had a second child born out of wedlock. Most of the girls were embarrassed to return to school, and those who did created a problem by talking too freely about their escapades. Consequently, the school officials, with the help of private funds, started a project to provide vocational training for the unwed mother—in dressmaking, beauty culture, baby care and office work. The project has a nursery attached where mothers leave their babies while attending classes but where they can go when their infants require feeding. While they learn to take responsibility for their children, they also learn a salable skill. The whole project is under the supervision of a director who helps the girls plan their futures.

Programs like these in delinquency prevention are far too few in the United States. A few school systems have been imaginative enough to set up projects to deal with kids who don't conform to the usual standards, but there are not many. Since schools are one agency of society that touches the life of every child in his most formative years, and through him his family, most schools could do much more in spotting delinquency and setting the wheels in motion to curb it. Very few delinquents who turn up in court at fifteen, sixteen or seventeen arrive there as a result of a single act. Offenders are rarely created overnight. Mostly, they have a long history of misbehavior which was first noticed at nine or ten years of age in the schoolroom, but nothing was done about it. With the proper facilities, most of our delinquents could be pinpointed and set straight before they got too deeply involved.

This will not be accomplished, however, merely with counselors and case workers. These are important, of course, especially for the maladjusted youngsters with home problems, medical problems or personality problems. But what is even more important is to have basic educational, or training, alternatives for that percentage of our children who do not fit into the conventional picture—the non-learners who find it hard to work with books.

"So long as the school lacks a varied curriculum to meet the needs of *all* youngsters," says Dr. Kvaraceus, "the effectiveness of the counseling, the social work, the psychological and attendance services will be severely circumscribed."

In sum, our schools are potentially one of our best weapons in the fight against delinquency. But they often lack the funds, the imagination, the public backing, or all three, to do the job. In effect, as far as the country as a whole is concerned, they have been warring with popguns rather than with heavy artillery.

12

WORK—EUROPE'S
NOT-SO-SECRET WEAPON

SIGMUND FREUD said there were only two realities in life—love and work. I don't know how much our teen-age delinquents are getting of the former, but I do know they're getting precious little of the latter.

Last June on the island of Manhattan, school let out, and thousands of youngsters rushed to get summer jobs. Few succeeded. The rest watched TV, visited the playgrounds, badgered their families for pocket money, walked the streets, went to the movies and took the subway to the beach. Some hung out with gangs. A few studied. Most were bored. If they watched TV, they were told endlessly what cigarettes to buy, what cars to buy, what beer to buy. Buy . . . buy . . . buy. With what?

It was bad enough for those interested in school and ready to go back in the fall. But for the near-million across the country who had just dropped out because our school curriculum had nothing of interest for them, prospects were gloomy indeed.

"Among these dropouts we find the discouraged, the aimless, those without purpose, often killing time while awaiting the call to military service," says Joseph Lohman, Chicago's studious ex-sheriff. "In this group, we find the overwhelming majority of the juveniles who steal 70 percent of all the cars stolen in the United States, as well as those responsible for the alarming upturn in vandalism."

Over and over again, I heard people who work with delinquents on a day-to-day basis—gang workers, police, judges, school counselors—urge that something be done to get jobs for our idle youngsters. Even social workers, who a generation or so ago were urging the passage of child labor laws to keep kids *in* school and *out* of industry, are now doing an about-face and pushing for some revision of those laws in order that certain youngsters may leave school earlier and go to work.

Although children in most states are able to get working papers at sixteen, management is rarely interested in hiring them at that age. There are too many restrictions. A child of that age may not be worked in certain places, he may not be allowed near certain machinery, he may not be kept overtime, etc. Insurance companies make certain demands when children of this age are employed. In short, it is much easier for management to wait until the youngster is at least eighteen.

On the other hand, unions are even less interested in seeing that such youngsters have work. They take a dim view of accepting under-eighteen members, even for apprenticeship. There are *only five,* out of 120 trades, for example, where a youngster without a high school diploma can qualify for apprenticeship training.

Let's look at Joey—a typical Manhattan boy of seventeen. Joey was not very interested in school, and dropped out at the first opportunity. Out of boredom, he joined a gang. However, one of the Youth Board's street workers wooed him away from gang life to the point where he was anxious to get a job and lead the life of a normal citizen. For three months Joey worked with enthusiasm in refurbishing a settlement house—all without pay. In the process, he became so skillful with woodworking tools that it was obvious he could, with a little training, become a first-rate carpenter. The street worker found him such a job, but when Joey revealed he was not a member of the union, the employer refused to hire him. At this point, Joey went to the union, but they told him they couldn't take him unless he had a job. To the youngster, it looked as though society were giving him a runaround, and Joey was bitter about it. When I last heard about him, the street worker had turned up a job pushing a hand truck through the streets of the garment district, but this wasn't what Joey wanted to do. His natural talents were going to waste, and he knew it.

It is amazing what a few jobs in the community will do to the delinquency rate. During the 1958 newspaper strike in Philadelphia, citizens suddenly found themselves unable to pick up their daily newspapers at the usual stands. Then, in a classic example of free enterprise, a bunch of youngsters rushed down to the newspaper plants, picked up the newspapers, and hawked them at railway and subway stations for ten cents instead of the usual five cents. They did a brisk business. During this period, the police were astonished to notice that there was a sudden and mysterious drop in the usual theft of parking meter coins.

Kids themselves often cite the lack of a job as one of the reasons for getting into trouble. Not long ago, 486 youngsters doing time for serious offenses at the State Correctional Institution at Camp Hill, Pennsylvania, were interviewed in depth as to why *they* thought they had run afoul of the law. The majority stated that, although they came from communities that had adequate athletic and playground facilities, they felt that enforced idleness was the principal factor in their getting into trouble.

It is interesting to note, furthermore, that most of these boys had poor school records. They were not interested in what they were being taught, and many felt they would have done better in vocational shops, gymnasium work, typing, etc. Three-quarters were truants who said they were sure they could have obtained work if they hadn't been compelled by law to remain in school.

Dr. James Short, of the University of Chicago, says, "We're soft on work in this country. We pass child labor laws to keep kids out of dangerous jobs, and then we overdo it to the point where there's little of *anything* for them to do."

Short, incidentally, is among those who believe that the striving for status is the biggest cause of delinquency, but he also admits that a job offers the quickest way for a kid to gain status and climb out of the adolescent limbo.

Judge Mary Kohler, the practical ex-juvenile court judge of San Francisco, also agrees that money earned from a job is the best status builder, and suggests that some sort of junior apprenticeships be made available at small pay for those youngsters who are not interested in school. Such training opportunities, she believes, could be built right into our school system.

"In our type of mass education," she declares, "we act as though there's only one type of learning—book learning. Let's face it; some people learn best in other ways."

Those who have attempted to do something about creating work for juveniles not interested in school—like Philadelphia's experimental Youth Conservation Corps—have usually been able to work out something eventually with labor unions at the local level. However, organized labor at the top level has little sympathy for this type of project. In general, I found labor was *not* sold on labor as a deterrent of delinquency.

"The idea that work is the answer to juvenile delinquency strikes me as complete nonsense," Alvin Zack, spokesman for the AFL-CIO, told me flatly in Washington.

His point of view was echoed by another high labor spokesman in New York—Leo Perlis, director of the AFL-CIO Community Services Activities, a branch of labor directly concerned with the problem of juvenile delinquency.

"Work for the young, in itself, does not prevent delinquency," he asserted in a speech before the 1960 White House Conference on Children and Youth. "The wrong kind of work in the wrong kind of environment often promotes it," he added, citing the case of a twelve-year-old girl who was caught and killed in a potato-digging machine on an Idaho farm, although exactly what this tragic incident had to do with juvenile delinquency he did not make clear to his audience.

This same policy speech offered as one of the reasons for delinquency the "fact that one-fifth of our nation is ill-fed, ill-clothed and ill-housed." According to this line of reasoning, the delinquency rate should have been much higher in the days of the Depression when *one-third* of the nation was ill-fed, ill-clothed and ill-housed. All statisticians agree, however, that at that time the situation was exactly the opposite: delinquency rates were far lower.

In general, organized labor's concept of delinquency is fairly close to that of most of our sociologists, namely, that it's almost entirely a phenomenon of the lower classes, and that the eradication of slums, the abolition of poverty and a greater measure of prosperity and higher wages for all will do the trick in preventing it. They do not seem to realize that their formula, however praiseworthy in social terms, has not done much to curb delinquency in those places where such goals have already been won.

Moreover, labor offers an argument which at first glance most people find hard to resist. "We have a huge unemployment problem among our adults," Mr. Zack told me. "We should take care of them before we worry about jobs for youngsters." Stating his firm opposition to any revision of our laws which would enable kids to leave school sooner and take jobs, he said, "During the next ten years, we've got to find 1,350,000 new jobs for those eighteen-year-olds and over who will be joining the labor force each year."

This, of course, is a valid point. But Europe has the same problem and is inclined to look at it differently. In those countries where delinquency is under control, they believe that a job or an apprenticeship—albeit a minor one with small pay—is as important to a certain child of fifteen, who is at a critical and formative stage in his life, as it is to a man of twenty-two, who has reached a certain maturity and is able to handle his problems in a more rational manner. For this reason, labor and management have joined hands in many countries, and both have agreed to "give" a little in solving their youth problems.

Let us look at Austria. Realizing that many boys are not academic-minded and should be started on their life's work, rather than some makeshift work, as soon as possible, the country has come up with an imaginative solution. They have created a string of "apprentice villages," which are in effect a kind of boarding school for youngsters more interested in working with their hands than with their minds.

I visited one of these "villages" outside of Vienna, a place called Jungarbeiterdorf-Hochlein, which is a bus ride from town. Actually, it is a lovely estate which once belonged to a rich coal magnate. On it there are a dozen or more houses, where several hundred boys, between the ages of fourteen and eighteen, live. Each day they go off to town or to nearby villages or factories for on-the-job training in the particular craft they have chosen. At night, they return home. They are not allowed to be away after 9 P.M. Once a month, they can have a weekend away, provided they have a definite invitation, and there are various other days they can have off in addition to Saturday afternoon and Sunday.

Every house, simple but cheerful, contains twenty-four boys in all, but is divided into apartments, each of which provides homelike living quarters for six boys. The house is under the direction of a young housefather, generally in his early twenties, who is apt to be a graduate student at the university. Such an arrangement helps the latter pay his way through college. Most housefathers stay about three years, or as long as they are in college. With this type of personnel, salaries do not have to be high, and the boys have the advantage of living with someone fairly near their own age but old enough to wield authority. The youngsters have the further advantage of coming in daily contact with a man of some intellectual background who also serves as a substitute father image. Each housefather, incidentally, has as assistants two older boys (seventeen or eighteen) chosen from the house. It is considered an honor to be selected, and in the housefather's absence they act as substitutes.

Austria's "apprentice villages" were started just after the war by Dr. Bruno Buchwieser, the son of a wealthy contractor, as an answer to the question of what to do with young boys, many homeless, who were not interested in school but who were, on the whole, too young and inexperienced for full-fledged jobs.

The concept grew, and at present the "villages" include some boys who've been in trouble with the law, some who have poor living conditions at home, but also many whose parents simply feel that their boys would benefit from the life and training which such places have to offer. Thousands of boys are enrolled in these "villages" throughout Austria (five thousand are in the Vienna district alone). The grounds, the buildings and much of the support comes from private sources—from individuals, from industry, from labor unions and from the church. One of the largest of the "villages," for example, was made possible by the generosity of the Society of Manufacturers, the equivalent of our National Association of Manufacturers. All boys are paid a stipend during their training, and are required to pay for their room and board. However, if the sum is insufficient to pay the full cost, the difference is paid by the parents. If they are unable to do so, then the state pays for it.

Spending a day in the beautiful setting of an old country estate, with its rolling hills and clipped soccer fields and tidy apprentice houses, each with its game room and its forest of skis stacked at the door, I had the impression one gets from visiting one of our New England prep schools. And the morale seemed every bit as high. The only difference was that in Jungarbeiterdorf-Hochlein, the boys were proudly graduating as auto mechanics or stonemasons or gardeners or shoemakers—"second-class citizens," if you will—instead of as candidates for higher education in some college or university.

One boy I talked to was typical. His name was Walter, and he had just turned eighteen. He was tall, blond and handsome, and he had been chosen as honorary assistant to the housefather for his final year at Jungarbeiterdorf-Hochlein. Walter had quit school in Linz at fourteen, quarreled with his mother and gone off to Vienna. There, he had drifted around for several months until someone told him about the "apprentice village." During his time there, he had been studying construction, and he had a job already lined up for the following year when he planned to be on his own.

Although Austria has the most attractive and well-organized apprentice villages, most other countries have made some provision for the nonscholastic type of youth who wants to work with his hands. In Germany and Denmark, as previously noted, boys are allowed to leave school at fourteen provided they enter into a definite form of apprenticeship, which is just as rigid in its own educational way as the most demanding academic high school course in this country. The training period lasts from four to seven years.

Italy's Boys Towns, started after World War II by the famous Monsignor John Patrick Carroll-Abbing to take care of Rome's homeless "shoeshine boys," has mushroomed into a vast network of nine Boys Towns, handling thousands of youngsters. They are, in effect, much like Austria's "apprentice villages." Some of the boys enter at ten or eleven, and stay until they are seventeen or eighteen. "The main thing is to teach a boy a qualified trade," insists Monsignor Carroll-Abbing, a dynamic Irishman and organizer who could certainly have been mayor of Boston or New York if he'd set his mind to it.

In addition to going to school, Boys Town youngsters are taught carpentry, ceramics, shoemaking, mechanical and electrical work, plumbing, gardening and many other useful trades. They are paid small sums for learning, and out of their pay they must reimburse Boys Town for their room and board. The surroundings are idyllic. Most Boys Towns are farms, where there are livestock, vegetables, fruit orchards and vineyards from which the boys learn to make wine. There are swimming pools, athletic fields and chapels as well. The system has proved so successful that not long ago a Girls Town was established under the direction of Mother Dominic Ramacciotti, an engaging and energetic Baltimore nun. Here, the girls, who enter at fourteen, are taught to be governesses.

Interestingly enough, these Italian institutions, which are primarily trade schools for the young, have been made possible entirely through the generosity of American contributors. Using U.S. money, the Italians have put into operation their own theories of child-raising—theories which it would be very difficult to put into practice in this country.

There is no way of telling if such methods have been responsible for the decline in Italian delinquency, but nevertheless the latest available figures show a decrease for the country as a whole. Despite an upswing in juvenile crime in the prosperous and industrial north, the over-all number of crimes for which juveniles have been convicted has dropped a substantial 14 percent in the last half-dozen years. This has happened in spite of a corresponding increase in the nation's population.

Some Americans who have seen Europe's apprentice programs in operation have come away with the feeling that work is the most important weapon one can use in the fight against youthful misbehavior.

Judge Kohler, who visited four European countries several years ago to study the situation for the Ford Foundation, had this to say about what she saw:

"One of the principal deterrents to juvenile delinquency in Europe appears to be the practice of sending young people off to work *when they are ready to work,* instead of forcing them to remain for an arbitrary period in the classroom where they move from boredom to mischief to real trouble. Soon they begin to associate with men in a productive enterprise. Soon they are accepted as responsible members of society, with all the respect and recognition that that entails. Thus fortified psychologically, they do not need to reinforce their self-esteem through gang activity."

Not long after visiting various apprentice-training programs abroad, I was in California, where I talked with Virgil Clark, the director of one of Los Angeles junior probation camps. I found him a strong advocate of revising our work and school laws so that certain students could be allowed to leave school at fourteen and pursue some other type of training. "We are hipped on the 'democratic' ideal of giving everyone an equal chance," he said, "but the way it ends up, certain kids just never get that chance."

Clark cited as examples two of his "alumni," both certified delinquents. One youngster, fifteen, got interested in plastering while at camp. He decided that he preferred that to study, and when released from camp, he tried to get a job in that field. He was, of course, too young even for consideration. He went back to school because he was forced to, and ended up failing every course that he took. Within five months he was back in camp for stealing an automobile.

The other youngster developed an interest in gardening while at camp. Fortunately, he was sixteen when he was released, and he was lucky enough to get a job in a nursery. He made good, bought his own car instead of stealing it, and the community had no further trouble with him.

"The trouble with our society," said Clark, "is that, generally speaking, we make no provision for the adolescent unless he plans to go to college."

Clark should have added, of course, "or unless he gets into trouble," because many states at the moment are operating forestry camps for boys who have committed offenses of various kinds. They are similar to the old Civilian Conservation Corps camps of the Depression. I visited a number of these in my travels, but one of the most impressive was in Pine Grove, California. The director of the camp, a retired Army major, W. S. Evans, told me proudly on the telephone in advance, "When you see the lack of tension among the boys after they're here a while, you'll be convinced of the worth of these camps." The major was right. The faces of the young men coming back from a day outdoors making firebreaks certainly didn't have the same expression such youngsters wore in juvenile court, just before being sent off to camp.

Our forestry camps are one of the few places where this country practices work as a therapy for the young, but unfortunately such benefits are available to youngsters only *after they become delinquent and after their sixteenth birthday.* At Pine Grove, seventy boys, many of whom have committed robbery or serious assault, spend an average of six to eight months out of doors, doing a full day's work, five days a week. They are paid fifty cents a day. Weekends are free, and they can have visitors at that time. The boys range from sixteen to twenty-one years of age.

In general, the forestry camp idea has proven successful. The work is healthy, the surroundings wholesome and the community benefits from the project. Unfortunately, however, unless one wants to spend his life as a forest ranger, the work does not lead anywhere. It is a means of getting boys off the streets and doing something worthwhile, but more practical-minded Europeans feel that for large numbers of boys the idea is a waste of time. They feel there is no need to train such a large corps of men in a skill for which most will have no use later on. They would rather put boys in an equally wholesome setting near some large city where there are opportunities for them to get on-the-job training in various crafts which they could practice when they got out.

At the time of writing this, various proposals have been made by our own government which would provide employment and training for our adolescent males who are not college-bound, but so far little or nothing has been done.

In 1961, the Kennedy Administration proposed the establishment of a Youth Conservation Corps which would be similar to the Civilian Conservation Corps of the Depression days. The plan calls for a program of 150,000 boys between the ages of seventeen and nineteen, who would volunteer for a year's service on conservation projects. Most people working in the delinquency field believe that such a program would be a step in the right direction, but that it does not go far enough. Such Youth Conservation Corps programs would have the weaknesses of the forestry camps: they do not get boys going on their lifework, but merely postpone the training which boys must get sooner or later when they start their regular careers. Another difficulty, from the delinquency point of view, is that the boys would be taken at an age when delinquency is beginning to taper off. The critical age for the type of boy who will be a Youth Conservation Corps candidate comes several years earlier, and is largely made up of school dropouts or potential dropouts.

Shortly after his Youth Conservation Corps proposal, President Kennedy proposed a three-year, $275,000,000 program which would benefit both males and females between sixteen and twenty-two years of age, and would include not only the Youth Conservation Corps but various "on-the-job" training programs, as well as "local public service and public works programs." The Secretary of Labor would be boss of the project. So far, however, nothing has been done about it.

That many high officials are concerned about the work opportunities for our nonacademic youngsters is beginning to be evident. Not long ago, Abraham A. Ribicoff, Secretary of Health, Education, and Welfare, came out strongly for a revision of our child labor laws to allow children a "valuable taste of useful, gainful employment."

Declaring that laws to prevent the exploitation of children might have become too rigid for their own good, Secretary Ribicoff said that present regulation would not have permitted him to hold any of the jobs which he himself had as a youth. The Secretary, for example, worked on a milk truck at twelve, in a garage at fourteen and as a member of a road construction gang at the age of sixteen.

In testifying before a Congressional committee considering a bill to combat juvenile delinquency, the Secretary declared that laws against child labor could well be a factor in the delinquency rate.

"We have too many laws that do too much coddling of children,"

he added. "There's nothing so valuable as useful, gainful employment for youngsters. There's nothing that will lift up a youngster's
sense of self-respect and give him a sense of responsibility."

This point of view is also echoed by a respected worker in the
delinquency field—Karl Holton, chief probation officer of Los Angeles, who has spent a lifetime working with youngsters. Specifically,
Holton pinpoints the critical age for males as between fifteen years
nine months, and seventeen years.

"This is the big danger gap," he says. "Kids are too young to get
into service, too young for apprenticeship programs, too young to
get anything but makeshift jobs. Many are big youngsters. They want
money. They're not interested in an academic career. The biggest
percentage of troublemakers come from this group."

Holton suggests that unions, industry and schools get together in
the community to set up "junior apprenticeship" programs for those
youngsters interested in working primarily with their hands. He believes that if such programs could be started early enough, the
youngsters in them would have sufficient incentive to get the academic training that they need.

"Leaving thousands of strong teen-age boys on the street without
opportunities to get apprenticeship training and the kind of education *they will take* is a tremendous waste of time and money," he
argues. "I'm not suggesting we have a return to the evils of child
labor, but there's an in-between. You don't have to throw the baby
out with the bath water. We make certain allowances for farm children in this regard. Why not for city ones as well?"

The English authorities strongly believe that, as soon as kids leave
school (and they may now do so at fifteen), some arrangements must
be made for their employment. It may be poor pay, at the bottom
rung of apprenticeship, but it's a start on a *meaningful* career that
can eventually lead to a good job.

"The English have the feeling that if the school lets the boy out,
then the economic system should let him in," explained a London
juvenile judge.

Robert Taber, the Philadelphia school official who has cooperated
in that city's experimental but successful Youth Conservation Corps,
also believes that it's crucial for youngsters to feel that there's an

unbroken line in the transition from school to job. Like Holton in Los Angeles, he believes that business and unions should get together to provide job opportunities "since delinquency, in the last analysis, is everybody's business."

"And if such cooperation does not produce these opportunities," he says, "then the government should step in and work out meaningful jobs in the community, by subsidy if necessary. Under our present system, there's a vacuum which delinquency rushes in to fill up."

13

Do Our Institutions

Manufacture Criminals?

It was late in the afternoon. I was almost in the shadow of the Pyramids, visiting the big Giza Reformatory in Cairo, Egypt. The story I heard there was straight out of Verdi, with overtones of an Islamic soap opera.

Aida had been sent to the reformatory when she was thirteen. She was homeless and she'd been in trouble. "She was not a virgin," Director Mostafa Hassanien delicately explained to me with nuances that indicated this was a wild understatement.

Like all of the twelve hundred boys and girls who are at Giza, Aida was given the usual tests and examinations and then assigned to a house, or "family," of forty girls. Each group has a "mother" and wears clothes with the special color of the house. Aida felt at home quickly and got on well. First she was taught to read and write, and then she was given the choice of studying sewing, housekeeping, embroidery or typing. She chose sewing. During the next few years, she acquired considerable skill at her craft. She also developed well physically, partially because of the extensive mass calisthenics which both boys and girls at Giza are required to do every day. And like everybody else, of course, she was allowed to go to the seashore for ten days of swimming and sunning and boating at a camp near Alexandria.

When she was almost eighteen years old and about six months away from being released, she was put on a semi-liberty basis—a privilege which most Giza youngsters earn. This means she was allowed to spend her days outside the reformatory, working in an underwear factory, but she had to come home to Giza at night.

While enjoying this new touch of freedom, the attractive, dark-eyed girl met Khali, a twenty-two-year-old young man who also worked in the underwear factory. They fell in love. Presently, Khali visited Giza's director and asked if he might marry Aida when her time was up. Director Hassanien said he would see about it.

During the next few weeks, the head of the reformatory checked into the boy's background as carefully as if he'd been her father. Eventually, he decided the match would be suitable. He then sent for Khali, told him that the girl was not a virgin, and, as he explained it to me, "I made him feel good about it." The boy was equally frank about his own problems. He had had a quarrel with his father, and the two of them had not spoken in several years. Parental feuds are considered serious in Egypt.

When it came time for the wedding—the day after Aida's release —the ceremony was celebrated in the institution with the house-mother, teachers, officials and inmates attending. It was a bang-up affair, as Egyptian weddings are apt to be. The young man had contributed twenty Egyptian pounds toward expenses, and the reformatory had put up thirty. When it was all over, the newlyweds went home to a little apartment, for which all the furniture had been made by Giza boys in their workshops as a wedding present. That was a year or so ago. Today, the young couple often come back to Giza to pay a social call. Furthermore, one of the happiest results of the wedding has been some rehabilitation work that Aida has done on her own; she has restored the relationship that once existed between Khali and his father, so that the three of them now often have dinner together.

The thing that interested me about Aida's story was that it was not particularly unusual. Such things often happen in foreign reformatories. In general, it is far more difficult for children abroad to get institutionalized, but once they are, the authorities go to unusual lengths to see that they become normal, useful citizens again. And the recidivism records reflect this. Egypt, for example, is a poor country, but it has a sensitivity to the needs of children which results in various measures being taken which our institutions have either never heard of, do not wish to adopt or, most usually, say they cannot afford. Although generalizations may be dangerous, I came away with the feeling that most children's institutions abroad were more interested in rehabilitation and less in punishment than ours.

How different Aida's treatment was from that of a boy of fifteen I know, a youngster I'll call Eric. Eric lives in California, a state whose citizens have been extremely generous in providing funds for their juvenile institutions, more so than any other state in the Union. Last year, for example, the Youth Authority of California spent $15 million on new buildings alone. Certainly few communities in the world have money like that to spend on children in trouble.

Unfortunately, money isn't enough. Nor are buildings, as Eric found out. An unwanted child among five children (his parents admitted this later to the probation department), Eric soon got their message, and behaved accordingly. Finally, he found life so untenable that he decided to run away to his grandmother, who lived in another state. When he was picked up by the police and returned home, his parents said that the boy was beyond their control and needed some discipline. The juvenile court judge who heard the case sent Eric off to a youth work camp, his first taste of the institutional approach.

There the youngster was subjected to a series of homosexual advances from other boys. He didn't respond. In fact, he fought with whoever approached him in this way. Finally, the camp director wrote a report to the juvenile court judge saying Eric was "not responding to treatment" and sent him back to the county jail, where he spent two more months waiting for his case to come up again. As it turned out, the jail was later condemned as unfit for juveniles. Eventually, the court sent him to a Youth Authority reformatory for two more months of study. As a result of this, he was finally placed in a foster home, where he should have been put in the first place. At present, he is doing well, but such is the cumbersome bureaucracy and lack of flexibility in handling children in this country that Eric was forced to spend eight months in jails, a reformatory and a work camp on a legal charge no more serious than running away from home. Although Eric spent some time in the imposing setup of a multimillion-dollar reformatory—a place bristling with psychologists and other child experts—the simple truth of the matter is that he would probably have encountered more warmth, understanding and common sense in a dilapidated Egyptian reformatory than he found here. It is small wonder that so few youngsters are rehabilitated in our institutions.

Some foreign countries have developed a whole battery of tricks for handling children who get into trouble, things which do not exist here or are so little practiced as to have no effect on the total problem. In the United States, a child who is arrested and brought before the courts is either dismissed, put on probation or sent off to an institution. Except for a few forestry camps, there are no alternatives, generally speaking. If the youngster is institutionalized, he serves his term and then goes back home. And as statistics show, he usually gets into trouble again. He is then returned to the reformatory or training school once more. In the majority of cases, the American youngster turns into an adult criminal.

In other countries, alternatives have been developed to such a depressingly rigid formula. In England, for example, boys who get into trouble which is not serious enough for an institution but too serious for probation are sent to short-term "Detention Centers." Here, for perhaps ninety days, they go through something which can perhaps best be compared to the boot training which our enlisted men undergo. Hours are strictly regulated, everybody is kept busy, and there is an accent on spruceness, cleanliness and a certain amount of military drill. The results are sufficiently gratifying that Great Britain is increasing its facilities of this nature. The nearest thing we have to a short-term detention home in this country is the Highfields, New Jersey, project, and that is largely limited to one state.

Another trick up England's rehabilitary sleeve is the Attendance Center. For boys who get into trouble with the law, these centers deprive the youngsters of their weekends for a few months. Under the direction of ex-police officers, they report regularly to the centers, where they must spend their time doing physical exercises and learning some craft, like leatherwork or basket-weaving. "It has a certain nuisance value and it seems to work," says Dr. Emyl Hall-Williams, criminologist at the London School of Economics. "It's a little like being kept after school."

In addition, most Western countries have much more elaborate "after-care" services than we have. Our "after-care" service usually consists of seeing a parole officer once a week or once a month. Some parole officers have case loads as high as three hundred youngsters, and the best they can do is have parolees report by postcard. In other countries "after-care" is as carefully administered as institutional care.

In Egypt, for example, no child is considered released from an institution until he has satisfactorily completed a period of "after-care" as a regular citizen in the outside world. In this way, he can be returned to the institution if he does not make good without any further court order. The "after-care" treatment assists youngsters just out of institutions in getting jobs, a place to live, the right clothes and all the other things one needs to resume a normal place in society. And almost no institution I visited abroad would consider releasing a youngster unless he had assurance of a definite job or apprenticeship of some kind.

But aside from the treatment and other correctional alternatives available abroad, one of the outstanding differences between foreign countries and our own in rehabilitating youngsters is the size of their institutions. Just about every criminologist in the world agrees that the larger the institution, the more difficult it is to rehabilitate an offender. And yet in spite of this, we tend to build bigger and bigger training schools, reformatories and youth prisons. An exception to this is Highfields, whose director insisted on limiting the number to twenty boys—a stipulation that many believe has been largely responsible for its success.

Abroad, the tendency for years has been to make institutions smaller and smaller. In Sweden, for example, the largest institution has only eighty boys. And when I visited it, I found the director unhappy about its size. He considers fifty or sixty the right number. Consequently, he has broken up living quarters into cottages, each of which contains ten to fifteen boys. The institution, incidentally, cost $1,600,000 to build, and is only three years old.

In Denmark, no institution has more than a hundred boys. Mostly, they range in size from twelve to one hundred juveniles. In France, the largest I found was for 170 boys, and the director apologized for its size. He said he hoped shortly to reduce it to a hundred. In England, the *largest* borstal (a reformatory for young people between seventeen and twenty-one) ranges between two and three hundred, and many are smaller. In India, soon no institution will contain more than one hundred. In Austria, where most convicted juveniles are gathered in Kaiserebersdorf, a huge thirteenth-century castle outside Vienna housing several hundreds of youngsters, the authorities have created a feeling of smallness by breaking up the place into apartments for fifteen children each. Every apartment has its own housefather and its own special atmosphere—permissive, strict, intellectual, sports-conscious, etc.—to suit the needs of the child being handled.

Almost all our institutional heads admit that they cannot do an effective job with such huge establishments as we have here, but at the same time they say we cannot afford to build smaller ones. Superintendent Donald D. Scarborough, head of New York State Vocational Institution, at Coxsackie, New York, has eight hundred boys to look after, far too many, in his opinion, to do an ideal job. On the other hand, he says we'd have a "taxpayers' revolt" if we tried to build smaller places "since larger ones cost less to operate."

At the moment, over half our training schools have more than 150 children. Generally the number is much larger. In California, for example, the average size is between four and eight hundred. Deuel Vocational Institution, which I visited, has a capacity of nineteen hundred, and it was only a few short of this number when I was there. This elaborate setup cost $15 million to build, incidentally, and contains a million-dollar hospital—"the finest in the country," a supervisor told me.

In spite of all the opposition to larger plants, moreover, California is planning to build another with a capacity of 1,200. Eventually it plans to have a superplant of 4,800, consisting of four institutions of 1,200 each, built around a central core of utilities. "We'd have a lot of trouble on our hands if we spent the money it cost to build them smaller," says Heman Stark, director of California's Youth Authority.

Most people from abroad who have visited our institutions feel that their size is one of the important reasons for their failure. For, in terms of recidivism—i.e., the number of youngsters who fail to make good when they go outside and who consequently return to crime—we have failed indeed.

Accurate recidivism figures are hard to come by. Institutions are understandably reluctant to give them out. Furthermore, there is a disagreement about how long a person must refrain from crime before he is considered a recidivist, and many youngsters, of course, commit crimes for which they are never apprehended. However, on the whole, most authorities would agree that if a person refrains from crime for five years after being released he is not a recidivist. And on this basis, the rate of recidivism among our institutionalized youngsters would probably run between 50 and 80 percent. It is certainly over half. Joseph D. Lohman, an authority on the subject, says, "It has been established by numerous follow-up studies that between 60 and 80 percent of all releases from juvenile correctional institutions later establish adult criminal records." And Dr. Lloyd Ohlin, another respected researcher in the field, says, "No institution in this country can honestly claim less than 50 percent recidivism. With girls it's much higher."

It is also agreed that recidivism, on the whole, is far less in foreign institutions than it is here. Giza, for example, claims between 2 and 3 percent. English borstal rates, where accurate figures are fairly easy to obtain, run between 16 and 40 percent. In a comparison between the rehabilitation success in an English borstal and a Massachusetts reformatory made not long ago, the rate abroad proved *six or seven times better than ours*. Says Sophia Robison, in her book, *Juvenile Delinquency*, "There is telling evidence, in the high recidivist rate [here], of the ineffectiveness of most of our reformatories and institutions when compared with institutions abroad."

What then are the main differences, in addition to size, between foreign establishments and our own—differences that might offer a clue as to our poor record in rehabilitation?

Certainly one of them must be the length of time that a youngster is kept in one of our institutions. A recent report to Congress by the Department of Health, Education, and Welfare states that the average length of stay in our institutions is 9.7 months. In the rest of the world, it is apt to be much longer. Although, as we have seen, it is much harder for a youngster to become institutionalized abroad (they are more tolerant of deviant behavior there), once a child is finally taken away from society, *he is apt to stay there two or three years, long enough to learn a whole new way of life.* In an English borstal, for example, the average stay is three years.

At the Preston School of Industry, a comparable California reformatory that boasts among its alumni such celebrities as Rory Calhoun, Rochester, Caryl Chessman, Pancho Gonzales and Eddie Machen, the deputy director, Tom Montgomery, says the average stay of six and a half to seven months is too short a time to teach boys much of anything.

"We would like to keep boys longer," he says wistfully. "We feel we could really do them some good. But how can we? We're overcrowded as it is, and there are four hundred boys waiting right now to get into our state institutions."

The answer, of course, is that too many children are being picked up on too many trivial charges.

"In my opinion, we overarrest and we overconvict," says Roy Votaw, assistant director of the California Youth Authority. "In many instances a reprimand or a bit of counseling would do the trick. If we picked up fewer children and kept them longer, we'd probably have more success." His views were echoed by the Youth Authority's director, Heman Stark, who expressed alarm over the tendency of the courts to send more and more children to correctional institutions. "Ten years ago," he said, "12 percent of the kids who came before our juvenile courts were sent to institutions. Now it's 16 percent!"

Another crucial difference between institutions abroad and our own is their strong emphasis on work as a therapy. In this country, the tendency has been to move more and more in the direction of education and counseling rather than work training. Abroad, every institution I visited, without exception, considered learning a trade the central core of rehabilitation. "First we build a factory. Then we build a reformatory around it," explained a Danish criminologist.

In Austria, for example, a boy at Kaiserebersdorf is actually a fullfledged apprentice during his stay there. When he finishes, he takes his examination and receives a labor union certificate, if he passes, which never says where he has received his training—be he tailor, barber, plumber, butcher or gardener. The institution's workshops are excellent, and the teachers drawn from the best in the city.

Similar systems are followed everywhere. In England's thirty-seven "approved schools" (which are equivalent to our reformatories or training schools), the overwhelming majority have been recognized by the building trades as having proper standards for apprenticeship.

In France, *where the usual term at an institution runs three years,* a boy emerges as a full-fledged worker in his field, ready to take a job which the "after-care" department secures for him. Even in the French observation center at Savigny-sur-Orge, where youngsters spend only a short time while being studied for proper placement, the youngsters were spending half their time at welding, metalwork, painting, paperhanging, horticulture, stonemasonry and other trades. "We consider idleness the mother of all vices," the director said to me. Whether this approach to delinquents has any effect on national statistics would be hard to prove, but the fact is that the figures in France are going down. In 1949, 21,185 children were brought before the juvenile courts; ten years later, the figure had dropped to 18,900, despite a population increase.

In Germany, the Freiburg judge and juvenile authority, Dr. Wolf Middendorff, who recently completed a year studying United States institutions, said, "We consider work the main therapy in our institutions. When I visited a training school in Seattle, I saw all the youngsters watching television. When I asked the director what they were doing, he said they were occupied. 'How so?' I asked. 'Watching television,' he replied."

It is interesting that in Austria, for example, no television is allowed at Kaiserebersdorf. "Passive entertainment is not good," said the director. "We make our own entertainment—amateur theatricals, sports, etc."

In this country, everywhere I went I found a tendency to feel that work is not important. If it's done at all, it's apt to be done on a killing-time, rather than a serious, basis. "Work is not important," Jesse Adams, director of a Los Angeles probation camp, frankly told me. "It is only a tool. We teach work habits." His words were echoed by Wayne Harbert, of the Youth Authority. "In our institutions," he said, "we teach work habits, learning *how* to work rather than an actual vocation. We emphasize being on time, getting along with fellow workers, honesty, etc."

To a European or an Oriental, such words sound like mere sophistry. In their practical way, foreigners believe in getting a child going on his lifework as soon as possible. They feel it gives him something to cling to.

The American criminologist, Dr. John Conrad, who recently spent considerable time touring European penal institutions, came away with the feeling that we had no possible way of putting our kids at "realistic work" in our institutions.

"Frankly, our correctional plants are a mess," he said. "Work is manufactured. Kids are put at maintenance or made work, and they know immediately they're just wasting their time."

Dr. Conrad, like many others, is the first to admit, however, that there are many obstacles to changing our system over to a work-oriented one.

For one thing, most states have state-use laws which prohibit institutions from selling products made in training schools and reformatories on the open market. For another, labor unions are not interested in seeing that institutionalized kids get apprenticeships. ("With so many boys without police records waiting to get into our unions, why should we take in boys with records?" asks Joseph F. Burke, co-president of Pennsylvania's AFL-CIO.) Furthermore, our school and work laws discourage boys and girls from getting started in some trade at an early age. But last and most fundamentally, the real obstacle is that our authorities have not been sufficiently sold themselves on the idea of work as a therapy.

Certainly, there are institutions in this country that have no peer as far as equipment is concerned. A place like Deuel Vocational Institution—the huge, $15-million training school in California—has shops that would make directors of most foreign institutions pop their eyes with envy. Its weaknesses, however, were apparent from the moment I crossed the fence into the guardroom, greeted the elderly, uniformed man on duty with an amiable "Nice day!" and was greeted in return by a growling "What's good about it?"

For one thing, Deuel is too large—1,832 boys the day I was there. For another, it's too impersonal. Great cell blocks provide living quarters for 125 boys in each. Furthermore, the average stay is nine months, not long enough for a boy to get really launched on a trade. In addition, there is no selection of the type of boys sent to Deuel. The place is set up to teach highly skilled crafts, like airplane mechanics, and yet half the boys sent there do not have the mental equipment or educational background to profit from such technical training. Many, I was told, would make good farm hands. But although Deuel has a huge farm with eight hundred acres and three hundred head of cattle, *the boys do not run it* because the authorities fear they might run away if allowed outside the double fence that surrounds the main institution. One official told me in whispers that the place was too "custody-minded."

In the few cases where the proper boys fit into the proper slot at Deuel results are excellent. Welding and airplane mechanics, for example, can be taught without impinging on any state-use laws, and if the boys show any aptitude for this sort of thing, their rehabilitation rate is high. "A shop instructor can get closer to a boy than any other person in the place," the director said, "and can often have a profound effect on his life."

Such success, however, is apt to be limited. On the whole, Deuel is a perfect example of the failure of American institutions—too big, too impersonal, too short a stay, too much custody, too few boys being taught things they can do on the outside and, of course, too many boys who shouldn't be there in the first place. It is small wonder that Deuel's rate of failure is well over half: between 50 and 60 percent.

On the other hand, the same state that produced Deuel has also produced another institution—the Youth Training School at Ontario —which is a rare example of what such a place can be when people really set their minds to it. Recently built, it could well serve as a model for other such places across the country, and even penologists abroad had spoken to me enthusiastically about it.

Known familiarly as "Chino"* because it's near that town, the institution is large (1,200) but it is perhaps the first one in America dedicated to a *total* program of vocational training for everybody.

---

* Not to be confused with the well-known Chino Prison nearby.

What is more important, it is dedicated to the theory that *work must be the main therapy.*

Realizing that such a place would have considerable difficulty with labor and industry unless things were handled skillfully, Chino's planners did a thing which has been done in Europe for years: they brought both labor and management in on the planning at the beginning, and gave each a feeling it had a stake in the institution's success. Both groups were made to feel that delinquency in a community is everybody's business. Consequently they were eager to work out some solution. As a matter of fact, no one had ever approached them before. The concrete result was that a Trade Advisory Council for Chino was formed of thirty-six leading union and industrial men who gave advice on the most effective way of setting up the shops. Since the institution opened, these men have continued to meet every three months and give advice on technological changes, new methods of marketing and trends in employment for various trades. If the employment forecast looks promising in one field, boys are urged to go into it, and vice versa.

One example will show how useful outside advisers can be. Most shoe repair shops in boys' institutions teach how to repair men's shoes only. The Trade Advisory Council, however, came up with figures to prove that 80 percent of all repair work today is done on women's shoes. Consequently, the Chino boys working in this field are now strongly oriented in this direction. They do charity repair work for the Salvation Army and other similar organizations so as not to compete with the regular repair industry.

The whole institution is operated on a realistic basis. Boys do the maintenance work, but they get instruction at the same time. In the kitchen, for example, the cooks are not merely cooks; they are instructors, and all boys who work there learn the necessary skills. Janitorial work is done by instructors in building maintenance, with the help of boys who have chosen that field. Electrical and plumbing instructors hold classes in the mornings, and take their pupils out on jobs in the afternoon. All landscaping is done under the direction of teachers. Boys don't just go out and cut lawns. First, they have several hours of instruction on lawn-mowing machinery, or on plant diseases, or on how to graft roses. There are courses in carpentry, electrical work, masonry, plumbing, sheet metal work, shoe repair, building maintenance, welding, food preparation, painting and nursery work.

After studying a trade for a while, boys often realize that they need more mathematics or reading or writing, and they become sufficiently interested in getting it to go back to school and learn. Classes are available for such boys. A few of the latter have been able to finish high school and earn a diploma in this way, and when the state issues it, there is no mention of where it was earned. In all, Chino has fifty trade instructors and ten academic instructors.

One stocky, brown-haired boy I talked to in the kitchen was a typical product of the system. Recently turned eighteen, he had spent several months as an apprentice learning the art of vegetable preparation and cooking. He had shifted to baking a short time before, and at the moment I spoke with him, he was decorating a huge white cake with pink roses which he was squeezing out of a funneled bag with the delicacy and precision of a man bent on creating a masterpiece. He was enthusiastic about cooking—something he'd never tried before—and told me he hoped to get a job as a chef's assistant aboard a cruise ship when he got out. "I want to see the world," he declared. It was obvious he felt he had something to look forward to.

One of the advantages of Chino is its cost. Because of the fact that maintenance is largely done by the inmates, under instructors, the per capita bill runs to $3,098, somewhat less than it might be for a comparable institution elsewhere. On the other hand, its director, Lyle Egan, is not at all satisfied with its size, which he considers too large. However, an attempt has been made to create a more informal atmosphere by dividing the place into fairly small living units, each of which has fifty boys. Egan considers another Chino drawback to be the length of stay, which averages about nine months. "It's too short a time to complete an apprentice training, but at least we can get them interested," he says. "And it's hard to find a boy who doesn't have an aptitude for something, no matter what his I.Q. is."

A big problem, of course, is jobs. But because of the interest of both labor and management through their membership in the Trade Advisory Council ("Each one thinks he owns the place," confided a Chino official), the boys do far better than they would in most

institutions. Egan estimates that perhaps 75 percent of the "gradu-
ates" have some kind of job lined up before they leave.

Everybody connected with Chino is optimistic about the results.
When I visited it, the institution had not been operating more than
about a year and a half, and so it was impossible to get any valid
recidivism figures. However, of 333 boys released since it started,
only ten of them had been returned to court. This is a remarkable start
for any institution. Furthermore, during its first year of operation, only
three boys had attempted to escape—a record any place its size would
be proud of.

In view of such happy results, I asked Egan when I left, "Why
hasn't someone tried to get an institution like this started sooner?"

Egan shook his head and said, "I don't know."

Unfortunately, the story of correctional institutions in America is
not simply one of well-equipped plants, poorly or unimaginatively
used. In many places, the establishments are run-down, crowded,
badly staffed or worse. Many of our so-called training schools have
equipment so outdated as to be practically useless. One Midwest
institution of enormous size has but one engine in its motor workshop
—a Model A Ford—on which boys can work. There is no money to
buy anything better. And in the case of an Indiana reformatory, where
a General Motors executive had donated a new automatic transmis-
sion, the piece of machinery was still sitting there a year later, un-
used, because no one had incorporated it into the training system.
"There isn't anybody on the staff well enough acquainted with that
kind of equipment to teach it," I was told.

It is not surprising, all things considered, that when foreign penal
authorities visit this country they often go away unimpressed, feeling
that we do not do very much for our children once they get into
trouble and have to be put into institutions. "To be honest, I have
the impression your youngsters in training schools just sit, smoke and
look at television," said Karen Berntsen, of Denmark's Youth Clinic,
who had recently made a tour of this country.

With our unfortunate tendency to overconvict and overinstitution-
alize, with our reluctance to keep really delinquent youngsters long
enough to teach them a new way of life, with institutions that are

too large and too cumbersome to provide the kind of homelike and informal atmosphere penologists agree is necessary in order to rehabilitate, with our unwillingness to teach a child a trade so that he has something to fall back on when he gets out, with our reformatories and training schools often too far from big cities to attract good trade teachers or to arrange for apprentice setups, with no semiliberty status to help the inmate get gradually adjusted to normal life, and with inadequate "after-care" to help him slip back again into society, it is not surprising that so many youngsters who get a taste of our institutions are, like narcotics addicts, hooked for life.

"In unison, the police, the courts and the penal institutions often maladjust the young person so seriously . . . as finally to confirm [him] in a life of adult crime," says Joseph D. Lohman.

We know that under most circumstances the best thing to do is to keep a youngster away from an institution as long as possible. But when it *is* finally necessary to put him away, there's no reason why a community cannot have at its disposal an institution like Chino (only smaller), or indeed any number of other alternatives which might do the trick even better for the youngster involved. There's no reason at all why a child, once condemned to an institution, should, in our rich country, have a poorer than fifty-fifty chance of becoming a normal citizen again.

When all things are considered, it's not so surprising, after all, that the elderly guard at Deuel, when confronted with a "Good morning!" should have growled, "What's good about it?" From his point of view, in the middle of one of our overgrown correctional institutions, it probably didn't look very good. And from the average citizen's, or taxpayer's, point of view, it shouldn't look very good either.

14

WHY NOT TRY PROBATION

INSTEAD OF INSTITUTIONS?

IN view of the dismal lack of success when youngsters enter our institutions, the obvious question is: Why not put them on probation instead?

Probation is a system whereby specially trained officers are made responsible for the good behavior of children who come before the courts, in lieu of sending them to an institution. For a specified period of time, the youngsters must report regularly to such officers and are not allowed to do certain things—like leaving the community—without permission. If a child on probation does violate the regulations, he can then be sent back to the court for sentencing to an institution. A good probation officer, of course, does much more than just keep an eye on his charge's behavior in a negative way; he counsels him, gets him a job, arranges for medical care, acts as a substitute parent, etc.

Wherever probation has been tried *on an adequate scale,* the results have been stunning. Not long ago, in a three-year experiment in Saginaw, Michigan, the use of full probation facilities cut the number of persons being sent to institutions in half while the number of arrests remained the same. In effect, the evils and the cost of locking people up were reduced enormously, and crime did *not* rise. Since it costs about one-tenth as much to supervise a person adequately on probation as it does in a reformatory or training school, it's easy to see the advantages to a community on a cost basis, to say nothing of the advantages of keeping a kid away from the recidivism perils of a lockup.

Although adequate statistics are hard to come by, a recent three-state survey showed a recidivism rate of 20 percent for probation. Most authorities would agree, I believe, that the rate varies between 10 and 40 percent, according to the kind of probation services available. In view of these results, it is not surprising that Negley Teeters, the Temple University sociologist, says of probation, "It's the only answer to reformatories and training schools."

As things now stand, almost no community has adequate probation. "Probation and parole [the latter is the name given to the service *after* a person gets out of an institution] exist in name only in this country," says Joseph D. Lohman. One could easily say of probation what has been said of Christianity: it has never really been tried.

There are at present about 3,500 probation officers for juveniles in the United States, and it is estimated by the National Council on Crime and Delinquency that another 7,220 are needed immediately if *minimum standards* are to be met. Unfortunately, only about half the counties in the nation have any probation services at all, and those that do are generally understaffed. The National Council, for example, recommends a case load of no more than fifty youngsters for each officer, and yet the average runs about three times that. Some probation officers have as many as four hundred cases to handle. At present, the average time that an officer can spend with a child is *less than one hour per month*, and in some places, as I have said, the only contact is by postcard.

In Philadelphia, where the League of Women Voters made a survey on the subject, they found that 80 percent of a probation officer's time was taken up with writing reports, keeping records, preparing backgrounds of cases for court, etc. Only about 20 percent of his time was available for the all-important personal supervision of the youngster. Although case loads in that city average seventy-five, it is estimated that each child on probation spends only from fifteen minutes to an hour per month with each officer. In most of the rest of the state's counties, probation is just a token gesture.

One of the reasons for the scarcity of probation officers, of course, is the pay. Jobs often go begging because the average annual wage is $5,300, despite the fact that qualifications are stiff (often six years of college). It is not surprising that there has not been a rush to fill vacant jobs. In Europe, the pay is far higher, when one takes into consideration the cost-of-living differential.

To an outsider studying the probation system, one curious thing about it is that it has found so little acceptance in a country that invented it. For it was in Boston in the nineteenth century that a shoemaker by the name of John Augustus, shocked by what he considered the severity of our criminal procedure, launched modern probation. One August morning in 1841, when he visited court, he saw a wretched-looking drunk being hauled from the lockup and placed before the judge. Something about the man made him feel the fellow could be saved, and Augustus pleaded with the judge to put him in his charge for three weeks instead of sending him to the house of correction immediately. He pleaded so eloquently that the judge granted his request. Three weeks later, when Augustus returned with his charge, the latter was unrecognizable. Instead of a ragged, shaking wreck, he was clean, sober, neatly dressed, and he held his head up. Accordingly, the man was charged only with costs, and the case was dismissed.

From this challenging beginning, the idea of voluntary sponsorship of prisoners by interested laymen began to take hold. This continued for some time. Then, in 1867, Massachusetts passed a law providing for public officials, rather than volunteers, to be responsible for the supervision of juvenile delinquents. The idea of using professionals rather than amateurs gained ground, and today every state has some form of professional probation, however abbreviated.

Volunteers, on the other hand, are practically nonexistent. The nearest thing we have to a national voluntary probation service in this country is the fifty-nine agencies who comprise the nationwide Big Brother movement. Starting in a New York City church shortly after the turn of the century, this group now has between seven and eight thousand members, each of which acts as a sponsor, mentor and friend to a boy, usually fatherless, between the ages of eight and seventeen. Unlike probation officers, Big Brothers have no official status, are not paid, and anyone can become one, provided his background is wholesome and suitable.

Big Brothers have undoubtedly been helpful to the majority of the 126,000 boys whose lives they have touched since the movement was launched almost sixty years ago. However, they do not begin to reach the many thousands of delinquents who might be kept from our institutions and prevented from falling into a life of crime by a really adequate probation service—perhaps the one single service that would do more to control delinquency, once a child gets to the court stage, than any other.

It is paradoxical that as professional probation took over and the nonprofessional kind tended to die out in this country, other countries became more and more interested in the voluntary method. Faced with many of our own problems—large case loads, little personal contact, inadequate training, etc.—people abroad decided to solve them by going back to the lesson taught by the Boston shoemaker. Most countries I visited have developed a large corps of amateurs, some of whom are paid small sums. In this way, countries with little money for highly trained people have been willing to settle for second-best by tapping that large supply of civilians everywhere who love children and are willing to help if someone will only ask them.

The idea of supplementing our regular probation officers with volunteers has, of course, been suggested many times, but each time it is defeated, mostly by professionals who feel that laymen shouldn't be meddling in a business which, they feel, only experts can handle. They insist amateurs can do more harm than good. In Europe and the Orient officials acknowledge that this is a possibility, but in their practical way they feel it is better than nothing. "In many cases, they fail," says Madame Simone Mazel, a professional probation officer I talked to in France, where a sizable group of volunteers exists. "But on the whole, we feel they do far more good than harm."

The big advantage of a volunteer, naturally, is that his case load can be small, anywhere from one to five. With, say, an average of only two or three children to see, a volunteer can spend several hours a week with each one, instead of fifteen minutes a month, as many of our professionals do. Moreover, many people believe that such laymen can often achieve superior results. Major Evans, head of the

Pine Grove Forestry Camp in California, is a strong advocate of the volunteer system being adopted in this country. "Laymen," he insists, "get closer to boys than professionals. They talk the same language. They don't have preconceived notions about boys, and they don't talk down to them."

In Europe, most volunteer probation officers have a sort of semi-official status. They work directly under the permanent ones. In Denmark, for example, the ratio is about ten volunteers to every professional. They are paid by the state, but the amounts are just about enough to pay car or bus fare when they take one of their charges out. In Sweden, a volunteer, who is apt to be a young clergyman, teacher or farmer, handles from two to five cases at a time, and gets a token payment of two dollars per month per case. In France, they are paid nothing, but, as in all countries, it is considered a mark of prestige to be chosen for such work.

Madame Mazel, whose office is in Paris' Palace of Justice, has 120 delinquents on her roster. She told me that she didn't know what she would do without the help of her volunteers. Anyone in France can volunteer, she said, and, after an inquiry into his or her background, may be appointed. "Some are wonderful," she declared. "They work with the heart!" Her best volunteer is a middle-aged spinster (fifty-five) who works as a secretary and lives with her mother in the suburbs. "She works with both boys and girls and she never fails," said Madame Mazel. "She has the touch."

Another good volunteer, in the opinion of this French official, is a male elementary school teacher, forty years old, married, with two children of his own. He is a captain in the army reserve, has an attractive home, a little car and a small studio where he does amateur sculpture. "It's very important to have a mature man like this who has a good life and has gotten it honestly," said Madame Mazel. "He's also a poet and a musician—a well-rounded, good image of a man." On many occasions he takes his probationees on hikes over the weekend in the mountains. "It's hard to be a delinquent when you see a sunrise in the mountains," she added reflectively. "Yes, we want to keep our volunteers."

Austria is also enthusiastic about its volunteers. A few years ago, with no money to organize a professional probation service, the government decided to set up a voluntary one under the direction of Dr. Sepp Schindler, a psychiatrist. The latter got together a group of people who had full-time jobs but were interested in children, and turned them into part-time probation officers. He meets with them once a week to discuss difficult problems and how to handle them. Each volunteer works with from three to five youngsters, and is paid a small sum for his efforts.

So far, the results have been heartening. At the time I talked with Dr. Schindler, the system had been operating four years, and the success rate among the delinquents assigned to volunteers was 92 percent. Even if the country is able to afford a full-time professional corps, Dr. Schindler would like to keep his amateurs too. "They seem to get closer to youngsters," he said. "Children know that the volunteers are part-time, that they're working in other jobs, and they respect them for what they are doing."

Incidentally, one Austrian volunteer did his job so well that there were amusing aftereffects. He reformed a teen-ager who had a bad drinking problem so successfully that the boy, in turn, tried to reform his father and older brother, both of whom had a similar attachment to alcohol. The older men were furious. One day the probation officer had occasion to visit the boy's home because the youngster was sick. When the father realized who the visitor was he threw him out of the house. "You are the man who ruined my son!" he roared.

Of all the countries I visited, however, the most widespread voluntary probation service was in Japan. In this country, which has had a tremendous delinquency problem since World War II, the professional probation people have been unable to keep up with their case loads, which now average 285 youngsters each. And the Big Brother movement, which has more members in Japan than in the United States, has been unable to cope with the problem either. Consequently, the government, under the Ministry of Justice, has organized a voluntary service which now numbers fifty thousand members—the largest in the world. Each volunteer has an average case load of 3.3 youngsters, and receives a token payment of fifty cents per month per child.

In Japan, anyone who wants to be appointed a voluntary probation officer may apply through the mayor of his district. His application is then forwarded to the Probation and Parole Supervision Office, which checks into the moral background of the volunteer. If the checkup is favorable, the applicant is appointed for two years, and the appointment is renewable. It is an honor to be chosen.

As in other countries, these volunteers work directly under the supervision of professionals. They also have a semiofficial status. Unlike the Big Brothers, they have the authority, for example, to investigate cases.

Not all Japanese volunteers are unqualified successes, of course. Toshio Suzuki, a public prosecutor in the Ministry of Justice, told me that many of them are too moralistic; they have a tendency to lecture their charges. Some are worse. One, for example, told a possible employer that a youngster who was being considered for a job had been in an institution, although it was not necessary to reveal this. Another tried to extort money from parents.

But such things are rare. On the whole, Suzuki estimates that volunteers have only 10 percent failures, and, if this estimate is correct, it would mean that amateurs achieve results as good as the professionals, although the latter, of course, tend to handle more difficult cases. Suzuki is completely sold on the idea of voluntary probationers. The only drawback, in his opinion, is that they do the job so well that the government is reluctant to vote funds for the professionals.

Many people in the United States, of course, are also enthusiastic about the idea of voluntary probation as a supplement to our professional services. Among them is Milton Rector, the head of the National Council on Crime and Delinquency, perhaps the leading organization responsible for setting standards in the field of juvenile services.

"There is a definite place for the volunteer in our system," he says. "Unfortunately, as our educational qualifications for probation officers have risen, the volunteer became a threat to the professionals and was eased out. Consequently, we haven't done anything to develop volunteers."

One of the other stumbling blocks to using them is a certain public disillusionment in some cities over the whole method of probation, a disillusionment not warranted by the facts. Whenever a delinquent is brought to trial for some crime he has committed while on probation, the whole system is often attacked in the daily press. What is rarely mentioned is that the youngster on trial was never really given adequate probation treatment in the first place. More often than not, his only contact with the probation officer was a mail-order affair—reporting by postcard.

If we can't afford the kind of professional probation service a youngster in trouble with the law needs to get him going in the right direction, there seems little sense in not doing what almost every other country has done—organize a corps of volunteers to supplement our professionals. Even small payments for expenses would be worth it, especially when compared with the staggering cost of failure and of having to lock a kid up in an institution.

There is, moreover, a further dividend with volunteers. As many people have pointed out, we're not going to get far in fighting delinquency unless the whole community gets into the act. Voluntary probation has the advantage of getting ordinary citizens involved in a problem that is just about everybody's business.

15

SOME GOOD IDEAS THAT FEW,

IF ANY, AMERICANS TRY

IN the world-wide search for new methods to prevent, control and treat delinquency, people abroad often seem more unorthodox, more willing to try new things, than their counterparts in this country. One wonders whatever happened to the pioneer spirit that led Americans to develop the first juvenile court, the first child clinic and the first probation service in the world. The youth hostel, the after-care home, the halfway house, for example, have all been developed abroad recently in an attempt to devise a homelike atmosphere in which a child can work, live and study in partial, but not complete, freedom. In some cases, they are used *instead* of sending a youngster to a reformatory or training school. In others, they are used as a bridge to help a child back from an institution into the main stream of life.

This chapter will deal with a few schemes which are either operating with success in other countries or are operating here in a way that is far more limited than it should be. No scheme, of course, pretends to be a total antidote for the malady. It is merely one more remedy in the medicine chest.

THE BOSTON ATTENDANCE CENTER

In Chapter 13, I mentioned the British Attendance Center, a system whereby boys in trouble with the law are sentenced to spend their weekends for a few months at a place where they undergo physical exercise and learn some craft. What few people know is that the plan, now so popular that it operates in forty different parts of England, is really an American invention. It was borrowed from a Boston idea that has been operating quietly but effectively for many years. It came about as follows:

A little more than a quarter of a century ago, the recidivism rates at Boston's Juvenile Court were a shocker. A survey showed that 88 percent of the boys who passed through that court got into trouble again. On seeing the figures, Judge John F. Perkins called his probation workers together and insisted on a plan of action. The result was the Citizenship Training Group program, a scheme for boys who need *more than probation but less than custody.*

The plan is nothing if not down-to-earth. It insists that the majority of delinquents are not sick or emotionally disturbed, but are just badly trained. It does not theorize about who is responsible—society, the parents or the boy—but sets about the business of retraining the youngster *immediately.* The boy is committed within hours to a course which, he is told, he must cooperate with. If he does not, he will be returned to the court for resentencing.

Most boys cooperate, and the results have been exhilarating to the innovators. Now—twenty-five years after its inception—some 2,100 boys between the ages of twelve and seventeen have gone through the program. *Seventy-three percent of them have never gotten into trouble again!*

The training program is simple. It consists of a boy going to an old building on Boylston Street for two hours every day after school. There he does physical training, remedial reading (if necessary), arts and crafts, dramatics and singing. He looks at educational movies, and engages in other group activities, like going to camp in the summer. Excuses for nonattendance are not tolerated, and promptness is a necessity.

In addition, one of the first requirements is a complete physical examination. A few boys solve their problem right here. One Polish boy of fifteen, for example, had had his hand mashed and subsequently amputated as a result of an accident in a meat grinder. His career of delinquency and violence in school started soon after. The present director of the program, a youngish, energetic, ex-Army major by the name of Louis Maglio, saw to it that the boy was fitted with an artificial hand and given the proper counseling. From then on, the boy began to climb out of his delinquency spiral.

Mostly, solutions are not so dramatic. For the majority, it's a matter of redirecting and retraining a youngster's interest slowly. Some need a job, and here the C.T.G. tries to act as an employment agency. For others, it's a matter of family adjustment, or getting along with a group. The process is not accomplished overnight. The C.T.G. course runs for three months, and then the boy is returned to court. He may be reassigned to another three months on a full-time or a once-a-week basis. This may be repeated again and again. In some cases, the youngster may be a participant in the program until his eighteenth birthday.

With almost all boys, Maglio finds there's a natural aptitude for something. It's necessary to find what it is, and get the boy channeled in the right direction. One lad of fourteen, for example, had been making and selling zip guns to gang kids for five dollars apiece. His workmanship was impeccable, but his companions had made him impossible to manage at home. When the boy landed in the program, Maglio noticed his mechanical aptitude and arranged that he be provided with radio parts to fool around with. Before long, he was building miniature radio sets in soap dishes—even before the transistor was invented. "We encouraged him to get more education," says Maglio, "and today he is a successful officer in the Navy's electronics division, working on our national defense."

Some boys are statistical failures, but in the eyes of Maglio they are a success nonetheless. It is one of the reasons he is disenchanted with most forms of research in evaluating delinquency programs. One young man of nineteen, for example, who had graduated from the C.T.G. program four years before, was suddenly picked up on the charge of carnally abusing a child. Maglio was called, went to court and found his former charge—whom we'll call Don—full of embarrassment. The incident happened when Don and three other young men were on their way to a Saturday night dance. Halfway there, they were accosted by a fifteen-year-old prostitute, who looked much older. The boys took advantage of her offer. The girl never mentioned money until the affair was over. Then she demanded payment, which the boys refused. Furious, she went to the police and insisted she'd been raped. When the boys were picked up, they were charged with impairing a minor's morals. As a result of Maglio's intercession, Don received a two-year sentence, which was suspended. "Technically he was a failure," said Maglio, "but I consider him one of the best boys I've ever had." The young man, incidentally, is now married and doing well.

One of the advantages of the Boston program, aside from its high success rate, is that it costs only $300 per boy per year to operate, as opposed to about $3,000 if the delinquent is put in a reform school. In the case of the C.T.G., moreover, all the necessary funds are raised privately.

But in spite of these good results, the Boston program, like so many that originate in this country, has attracted few imitators. Why? Some think it's professional rivalry, others a devotion to vested interests, or an emotional attachment to one's own theories, or just plain jealousy. One researcher said to me, "How do you know it's successful? It's never been *really* evaluated. Sure, the juvenile court recidivism figures have dropped, but how do you know these boys haven't been rehabilitated by something else?"

One doesn't, of course. But the fact is that the court's success rate has gone sharply up—whatever the reason—and that's good enough for Boston.

THE GERMAN SHORT-TERM ARREST HOME

In their zeal to develop something between probation and the usual penal institution—a need which is acutely recognized but not generally acted upon in this country—the Germans have come up with the Youth Arrest Home. This is a combination of Boston's Citizenship Training Group program and Britain's Attendance Center, with elements of the latter country's short-term Detention Center (the brisk "boot camp" approach outlined in Chapter 13).

Germany has added some ideas of its own, however. For one thing, there is a wide choice of sentences. The youngster may be locked up (1) from one to four weekends, or (2) in a continual stretch from one to six days, or (3) in extreme cases up to four weeks.

Youth Arrest Homes are for boys from fourteen to eighteen years of age, and the treatment is harsher than that found in the English or American counterparts. Boys are kept in solitary cells, where they eat their meals and where they do some assigned work. The day I visited one of these places in southern Germany, the boys were pasting labels on commercial cherry brandy bottles. During the afternoon, the boys are allowed out of their cells for a short sports period, but they are not allowed to talk with one another. "If they do a little of it, we overlook it," the director told me. No smoking is allowed at any time, and there is no radio, television or movies.

There has been no research to prove the success or failure of Germany's Youth Arrest Homes, but the authorities are so convinced of their effectiveness that the treatment is now prescribed in *half of all the juvenile delinquency cases in which youngsters are found guilty.*

THE MORMONS' PROVO APPROACH

Outside of a few forestry camps, perhaps the nearest thing we have in this country to the Boston, English and German attempts to find alternatives to the probation-or-custody dilemma of our courts is an experiment being carried out in the Mormon community of Provo, Utah. There the program embodies some elements of all these attempts, with overtones of Highfields and its group therapy sessions.

Provo's remarkable young Mormon judge, Monroe Paxman, anxious to try out new correctional ideas, sentences certain boys to a period in which they must work part time for the city at fifty cents an hour during after-school periods and weekends. If they are not enrolled in school, they work full time. In addition, they must put in a daily stint at a group therapy meeting.

The work is of a clean-up nature, not unlike what the old Civilian Conservation Corps accomplished, and the discussion groups are under the direction of a Brigham Young University professor, LaMar Empey. The boys, however, are on a strict probation status, live at home and may be sent back to the court for resentencing if they violate the terms of their probation. At present, the whole program is being evaluated by the university's research staff.

One of the most controversial things about the experiment is that the boys are assigned to the program *on a purely random basis,* instead of being sent to an institution or put on probation. This highly unusual procedure for a court has been justified by Judge Paxman in the interest of science.

"I am not *sure* how effective a reformatory is, or even ordinary probation," he told me. "And so I'm using this method to find out whether one method is more effective than another."

His willingness to assign boys on such an unorthodox basis—a basis seemingly at variance with the usual concept of judicial procedure and one that has been criticized by the profession—is evidence that we still have some mavericks in the field who are not afraid to buck convention in trying out new methods.

THE HOSTEL OR HALFWAY HOUSE

In the United States, when a child gets out of a correctional institution, there is almost nothing available to help him fight the factors that got him into trouble in the first place, except, of course, a highly overworked parole officer. The latter, if he's lucky, can give him one hour of his time each month. Under such conditions, it is not surprising that Dr. John Otto Reinemann, director of probation for Philadelphia's County Court, recently returned from Europe with high praise for the "parole hostel" program which he found in England and Germany. This is a series of halfway houses where recently released juvenile offenders can find a new life in a substitute, family-type home. Twenty-six of these hostels already exist in England for both boys and girls, and even the city of West Berlin, fighting for its existence, has found the time and resources to establish one.

"Adapted to our own needs," says Dr. Reinemann, "it would be the answer to one of our big problems."

I visited a typical house of the type Dr. Reinemann describes when I was in Switzerland. It is located just outside Geneva and is called Les Ormeaux. It happens to be for boys who have committed some offense and are assigned there *instead of* to a reformatory. But exactly the same type of institution is also used for youngsters *returning* from institutions, and such halfway houses are found in France, England, Spain, Belgium, Holland, India and many other countries. The principle is the same everywhere: for a year or more, young people work outside during the day and come home to the hostel at night. They also pay for their room and board out of their earnings. In effect, it is not so different from Austria's "apprentice villages," except that in the latter the boys are generally not court cases.

Les Ormeaux is a big, attractive house of the type that so many rich people are giving up everywhere because servants are no longer available to run them. A suburban villa, it is only a bicycle or bus ride to town so that youngsters living there can get on-the-job training in stores, factories and offices. Jean Caviezel, an attractive young social worker, and his wife supervise Les Ormeaux, which houses fifteen boys between the ages of fifteen and eighteen.

One of the supervisor's duties is to help the youngster get a job, according to his talents and abilities. Each day, the boy goes off to his work, coming home for lunch. In the evening, the youngsters must be at home, but there is plenty for them to do. Les Ormeaux, for one thing, has a darkroom, and many of the boys have become interested in photography. There's also a machine and carpentry shop in the basement, and a library on the main floor. The inevitable stack of skis is close to the main door, for, in winter, the whole country becomes a sports playground.

All sorts of boys have been assigned to Les Ormeaux, including one who'd committed a murder. (He'd killed his father when the latter, drunk, was beating his mother.) And the recidivism record is remarkable. Only 4 or 5 percent ever get into trouble again with the law.

In India, I found many similar establishments. In the last several years, the country has started 135 after-care homes, each handling eighty-five or ninety children who are trying to work themselves back into the normal community life after a stay in a correctional institution. This struck me as remarkable for a country that is undergoing a supreme effort just to give its regular population the basic minimum of day-to-day necessities.

Often the physical setup in India is makeshift, especially compared to a rich country like Switzerland, but the results are excellent. Two years ago in Delhi, for example, the government wanted to open such a home, but funds were far from sufficient. The director appointed to do the job was not discouraged, however. He took over a gloomy, hundred-year-old city jail that had long since been abandoned. The children who were assigned to the home went to work on the jail and transformed it completely. Holes were patched, bars were removed, new glass was installed. Inside, white paint was applied everywhere to make the place more cheerful. Flowers and shrubs were planted outside, so that today the old jail looks like a villa in a resplendent garden. The cost was negligible, but judging from the low recidivism rate to date, the results have been excellent.

THE CHILDREN'S VILLAGE

A further development abroad has been another Austrian invention —the famous "S.O.S. Villages," or as they are popularly called, "the children's villages." Only twelve years old, they are already considered a strong delinquency prevention factor in a country where the delinquency rate is going down.

The idea of the children's village is to give young children in trouble a chance to lead a nearly normal life with a substitute mother, brothers and sisters. It is a cross between an orphanage and a foster home. It has the cost advantages of the former and the personalized care of the latter. The children in them may be in trouble with the law, they may have had a bad family life, or they may be orphans. But eight or nine of them, ranging in age from one to fourteen, are housed in one home with a "mother" who lives with them, cooks for them, disciplines them and sends them off to local schools if they are old enough.

The "children's village" was the brain child of a thirty-year-old Austrian medical student, Hermann Gmeiner, who set it up when he saw the living conditions of many children following World War II. He started his first "village" with only two houses. Each one was managed by a carefully selected housemother, dedicated to children. She did not have to wash clothes or mend or take care of major house repairs, but she functioned in every other way as the head of the family. She was given an allowance out of which she bought food, clothing and other necessities.

The idea was an immediate success, and today in Austria alone there are seven thriving "children's villages," handling thousands of children. The one I visited was in the Vienna Woods. It has twenty-four newly built houses, each contributed by some individual or organization. The setting, of course, is handsome, and the youngsters, when they come home from school, throw down their books with the same air of kids everywhere who are glad to be home. The preschool children romp happily in the ample gardens surrounding the various houses.

There is no trouble recruiting "mothers." Austria apparently has an abundant supply of single women who want to devote their lives to looking after children. The principal requirement, according to founder Gmeiner, is "a warm heart." For a few months, candidates for the job work as "aunts," helping "mothers" in other houses. Then, if they work out all right, they are given a house of their own. The turnover so far has been so slight that being appointed a house-mother has proved the equivalent of being given a lifetime job.

Austrians are very proud of their "children's villages," which are entirely maintained by private support. It is estimated that one out of every four Austrians voluntarily contributes toward their upkeep. One lovely Viennese girl, for example, who was a hostess at the Brussels World's Fair, met and married a rich young Belgian. When her father-in-law asked her what she'd like to have for a wedding present, she immediately suggested a house for one of the "children's villages." He sat down and wrote out a check for the cost: $20,000.

In Europe, innovations like the "children's villages" seem to have no trouble getting a speedy tryout in other countries. Although the Austrian idea has been operating only a dozen years and has not been buttressed by the elaborate research program that would probably be considered necessary here, the idea has already been taken over by Italy, France, Germany, Sweden and Belgium. In this country, an "expert" is apt to ask first: "But how do you *know* it works? Has it been proven scientifically?"

THE HOUSING UNIT SERVICE TEAM

Another idea that has been working well for years in England, for example, but has not been used here, is the Family Service Unit. This is a private, voluntary service which has been developed to help problem families when they move out of slums and into the big housing developments. It grew out of World War II when the Unit, consisting primarily of Quakers and conscientious objectors, did voluntary work relocating families bombed out by the Blitz.

Today, the Unit consists of teams of practical, noncritical workers who live in a house near a housing development and work directly with various families in need. A worker may spend a half-day or a whole day per week with each family. F.S.U. people *don't give financial relief,* but they know all about available community services and they don't hesitate to use them, if necessary. Mostly, they help a family by working right along with it. They care for children, help mothers with the washing, go to court if a youngster gets into trouble, do sewing, help paint a room, put up shelves, accompany a member of the family to a clinic, etc. They don't overawe their charges with interviews or advice, but they offer wahtever help they can on a sleeves-rolled-up basis. They are enormously effective with relief and "hard core" families.

"All kinds of things come up over a pile of laundry that would never come out in a formal interview," one of the Unit workers said to me, a cheerful, easy-to-talk-to girl of twenty-eight. She explained that she and her co-workers generally worked with a family for two or three years until the family had solved its most pressing problems and had managed to get on its feet.

The girl I talked to seemed more like a helpful member of the family than one's usual conception of a social worker. Later, the head of the Unit team in the area confirmed the reason for this. "We try to get practical workers, who get along with people and have an itch for service, rather than people who have a lot of degrees," he said.

At the moment, there are fourteen branches of the Family Service Unit in England, four of them in London. No definitive evaluation of its work has been made, but the London School of Economics has such a research project under way at the present time. The spread of the idea in England, however, is a reflection of the belief that the program has had considerable effect in cushioning the impact of families moving out of slums and into new housing developments, an impact which, as we have seen, often has disastrous effects here.

CITIZEN DELINQUENCY SQUADS

In a completely different category of delinquency prevention is an interesting idea now being tried simultaneously in Stockholm and Moscow. I don't know which capital had the idea first, but it consists of night patrol squads, made up entirely of voluntary citizens, who walk the streets and parks in an effort to discourage youngsters from committing delinquent acts.

In Sweden, the squad is usually a group of social workers appointed by the Child Welfare Board of Stockholm. They have no direct authority and they cannot insist that a child do what they ask. They merely talk to a youngster who seems to be getting out of hand—a youngster drunk, staying up late or committing an act of rowdyism—and try to persuade him to go home, to a welfare center or some other place where he will stay out of trouble. However, if the delinquent is defiant and needs curbing, the patrol can then call upon the city's authorities to take him into custody. Stockholm's youth has a name for these civilian patrolmen; they call them "baby sitters."

Moscow's equivalent is called the *Druzhiniki*. They have been described as a workers' voluntary patrol. The members wear red arm bands and function like a morals vigilante squad. Their very presence, incidentally, would seem to indicate a much larger delinquency problem than the Soviets are willing to admit.

The *Druzhiniki* have more authority than their Swedish counterparts. They have no power of arrest, but they do have the power to levy a small fine, which they seldom resort to. The *Druzhiniki* operate in pairs, and their tone is apt to be more evangelistic than punitive. They look on offenders as lapsed brethren who have strayed from the fold of Communist propriety and, like the Swedes, they tend to plead with misbehavers. They operate around the railroad station, where drunks and crowds are more prevalent, they drop into clubs where dancing is going on, etc. If a youngster gives them a lot of trouble, they can turn him over to the police, who will, in turn, give the name of the offender to his factory committee. The factory will take disciplinary action against him, or possibly against his father if the child is too young to have a job.

The authorities in both capitals seem to feel that civilian volunteers, patrolling the streets at night, not only can supplement a limited police force, but can offer advice and suggestions which are more acceptable coming from an ordinary citizen than they might be from a man in uniform. Moreover, since we supplement our police by using civilian volunteer patrols at schooltime to keep our children out of traffic troubles, there may be some validity in using similar patrols at night to keep our children out of delinquency trouble. There is nothing to prove that this will work, of course. It is merely a hunch that two European capitals are acting on, and it might be worth a trial in one of our own cities.

YOUTH FOR SERVICE

Another hunch that is being played—this time in our country—is in San Francisco. It involves the challenging notion that delinquents can be helped not by working *for them,* but by getting them to work *for others.*

Four years ago, Carl May, the Quaker building contractor who called a meeting of teen-age gangs on his own to iron out differences and also to arrange a dance despite police opposition (see Chapter 4), had an interesting idea. He had long been impressed with the work projects Quaker youngsters undertake voluntarily for the less fortunate, both here and abroad. However, these projects are done entirely by middle- and upper-class youth. May wondered if the idea might not work with boys in gangs and in the lowest economic stratum, thereby imparting the same benefits to the donors.

Through a contact in the Y.M.C.A., May got in touch with members of five of San Francisco's toughest gangs. They agreed to round up a group of gang kids at a meeting, where he broached the idea of their helping less fortunate neighbors by volunteering to paint and repair houses which needed it. The response was negative. "Nobody ever did nothin' for us, so why should we do somethin' for somebody else?" said one boy, summing up their reaction. Many of the boys were Negroes, and May decided to drop the idea that evening. He asked the boys, however, to meet with him in a week.

During that time, he organized a committee, and one of the members was the minister of a Negro church. The church needed to have some debris removed from its yard. It also needed to have a fence repaired and whitewashed, as well as a basement room painted for a children's recreation room. With the minister to accompany him, May went to the next meeting. This time he made his pitch for the church, and the boys hesitated. Finally one said, "If the other clubs will each send one or two boys, we will too."

The ice was broken. Since that time, four hundred boys, many of them with long records of delinquency, have completed 135 separate work projects in and around San Francisco, using their weekends to do so.

The projects have been both white and Negro. Generally, the boys are picked up early Saturday mornings in station wagons volunteered by members of the committee. They are then driven to the site of the project. They work in small groups (May found that when the groups are large there is too much horseplay), and they are given lunch on the job. In the past four years, they have washed walls, cemented parking lots, dug trenches, moved furniture, built septic tanks, hauled trash and repaired sinks and closets. Organized labor's reaction to so much unpaid work raised some questions at first, but May solved that by getting the secretary-treasurer of the San Francisco Building Trades Council, Dan Del Carlo, to serve on the committee.

One individual the boys helped was an elderly widow, not long out of a mental institution. She had been rejected by her son and daughter-in-law and, supported solely by Social Security, lived alone in a tiny house. She had no money to paint the house, which badly needed it, and the boys volunteered to take on the job. They were especially eager when they learned she had been rejected by her children. "They sort of look upon themselves as rejects," explained May.

It took four weekends to paint the house, but they were pleasant ones. The elderly lady made punch for the boys, and brought them cookies. They in turn went shopping for her. Just as the boys were finishing the job, however, the lady suffered a stroke. She was carried to the hospital by the boys, and died there two days later. All the youngsters attended the funeral. And after it was over, one of them summed up the feeling of all when he commented: "Well, at least she saw the house painted before she died."

On another occasion, the boys built a log bridge across a creek on an Indian reservation near Sebastopol, California. During the rains the creek was unfordable, and because of this a large area the Indians needed was uninhabitable. The bridge opened it up to them. The boys supplied the labor, but the whole community cooperated by donating hand tools, a chain saw, lumber, food and even a bulldozer.

May has called his project Youth for Service, and its effect on the four hundred boys involved has been electric. Although 75 percent of them had been in trouble with the law before the project got under way, few of them have been in any difficulty since. Some have gotten regular jobs. Others have gone back to school. And gang fights have become a thing of the past. Recently, the Ford Foundation was so impressed by the record that it decided to put $160,000 into the project. Part of the money will be used for a detailed study of the program by University of California researchers.

"In assisting the delinquent, we tend to do case studies or surveys *on* them, *to* them, *for* them, but seldom *with* them," wrote Dr. William C. Kvaraceus, the famous Boston educator, not long ago. "Yet no one can solve youth's problems for them. They must solve them *for themselves*." San Francisco's Youth for Service project, although limited in size, looks like a direct answer to Dr. Kvaraceus' words. It's a promising concept that's worth a try in more than one American city. Yet it has existed for four years without a flicker of interest in any other place.

There are other promising concepts, some modest, others more ambitious. Not all of them cost money, or very much, at any rate. But like the schemes just mentioned, they do cost ingenuity, imagination and the courage to break with the old methods and try something new. Some will undoubtedly work better than others in various localities. Some may not work at all. But most are worth giving a try.

16

IN CONCLUSION: DO WE WANT
TO CONTROL DELINQUENCY?

"WE have just as much delinquency as we want," said a wise Austrian who had been dealing with children for years. And although most of us would protest that we don't want *any* delinquency, the fact is that there's considerable truth in these words. We know enough about the problem to control delinquency to a far greater extent than it is now controlled. *But are we willing to pay the price?*

The price is not just a fee one pays for a prescription, and then forgets about it. Effective delinquency control is something that must be worked on constantly, and in those parts of the world where such treatment is a success the ordinary public is involved to a far greater extent than, it is involved here. It takes a many-sided attack to lick the problem, and most of us will have to get into the act, whether we're members of labor unions, businessmen, housewives, writers, doctors, civil service workers, churchgoers, etc. Are we willing to do that?

In this chapter, a number of action approaches are suggested. Some communities will find it useful to do some. Others will prefer others. But all must *do something* if delinquency is to be controlled. The problem cannot be met by letting George do it. Certainly the job is not going to be easy. And let us have no delusions about the enormous

pressures we are sure to meet from special groups who want to keep
the status quo as far as they are concerned.

Let us take an example of the kind of resistance one is likely to
meet. There is considerable evidence from the testimony of delinquents themselves that violence in the movies and on television helps
build up the problem, but as soon as measures are suggested to curb
it, the necessary controls are shouted down by the industry as socialism, Communism or just plain irrelevancy.

Again, although it is fairly obvious to disinterested workers in the
field that there is a close relationship between lack of a job and
juvenile crime, neither labor nor business nor even legislators want
to take the lead in doing something about it. It's easier to carry on
with the *status quo*.

If we are honest with ourselves, we know certain things *won't*
work. We know, for example, that eliminating poverty, building
new housing developments, creating more playgrounds, starting boys
clubs, passing curfew laws, stopping mothers from working, mending
broken homes, sending every kid in trouble to a psychoanalyst, cracking down on teen-agers, or going back to the rural life isn't going
to do the trick, even though some of these goals may be commendable
in themselves.

And we also know, if we are honest with ourselves, that certain
things *will* work. Aside from jobs, we know that good probation,
small institutions, better school counseling and curricula, adequate
medical service, better police and courts are effective in helping
youngsters in trouble. But we are often unwilling to provide the
funds that will make these benefits available. Although money is not
the only answer, enough is needed to provide minimum standards,
and this is usually not forthcoming. The fact is that many communities abroad, far poorer than we, spend a greater proportion of their
income on child welfare than we do. And as has been pointed out,
we prefer as a nation to spend the greater proportions of our income on highways, cars, cosmetics, tobacco, etc.

However, any realistic approach to solving our delinquency muddle
must be based on taking our society and our culture as it is. We are
not going to change it—overnight anyway. All those idealistic people who feel that the problem could be licked if there were a re-

birth of morality, or if all parents would take their responsibilities seriously, or if there were less emphasis on material goals and status-seeking and more on a return to the old-fashioned virtues (whatever they were) may be right. But they are also blowing smoke rings in a wind tunnel.

Let's face it: these goals are not likely to be achieved in a hurry.

There are, however, certain goals which can be achieved now—with a bit of effort—even in our present-day, supermobile, consumer-oriented, highly mechanized society. And most of them have been touched on in one way or another throughout this book. To sum up, the most important are:

1. *Work.* Although the reader has been repeatedly warned that there is no single panacea for delinquency, there are, of course, some remedies that are more effective than others. And if I were forced to select a single approach that struck me in my travels as coming closer to a whole solution than any other, it could be summed up in the four-letter word at the head of this paragraph.

It is easy, when one sees what has been done abroad, to feel that the principle of *meaningful* jobs for teen-agers, if applied here, could accomplish wonders. And yet work is the one therapy that is overlooked in this country. We prefer keeping our teen-agers on ice until they are eighteen or older. For those who are school-minded and can learn from books, the problem is not serious. But for the nonlearner, those two or three years of enforced idleness can be crucial. It is no accident that in this age group—fifteen to seventeen —we have the crux of our delinquency problem. As Secretary of Labor Goldberg has said, "There is a very real, very strong and very decided relationship between employment opportunity and delinquency!"

In this regard it is interesting to note the difference between two strikingly similar Scandinavian countries. In one (Sweden), the delinquency rate is soaring and may be the highest in the world, despite record prosperity and a quite astonishing distribution of material well-being for all. In the other (Denmark), the level of prosperity, culture and social betterment is roughly similar, but the delinquency rate is low. What's more, it's going down. Notice, however, that Sweden has a school-leaving age of sixteen. Denmark's is fourteen!

In the latter country, of course, leaving school must be accompanied by simultaneous enrollment in some sort of apprenticeship program so that there is no lag between school and work. In effect, the work is just a different kind of schooling.

Although it may be difficult to get our child labor and school laws revised to the extent of allowing certain youngsters to leave formal study earlier and take up some training program, it *is* possible (if this fails) to get started some program similar to Philadelphia's Youth Conservation Corps. With the cooperation of the schools, certain youngsters may be put to work part time and given academic credit for it.

The trouble with the Philadelphia Corps system is that the work, although better than nothing, is more or less meaningless as far as a youngster's career is concerned. But the fact that a community *could* get labor, the schools, the local government and the taxpayers involved in such an effort shows that the basic idea is possible. It can be built on.

Karl Holton, the head of Los Angeles' Probation Department, who has spent a lifetime working with children in trouble, feels that the biggest single contribution we could make to our delinquency difficulties would be to set up some sort of junior apprenticeship program. He believes it should not be for the bright, or even average, youngster who will become an aviation mechanic or some other highly skilled technician, the kind who generally ends up in our vocational schools. Rather, it should be for the less-than-average student who is not interested in a high school diploma, but would be interested in becoming a first-rate house painter, shoe repairer or maintenance man. He believes that students, enrolled early in such a part-time program, would do better in school because they would have more incentive.

To critics who insist that such programs, relegating certain students to less important jobs, is undemocratic or un-American, Holton retorts: "What's democratic about a school program that has little to offer this type of student, and leaves him idle, illiterate and without the ability to earn money in the richest society the world has ever known?"

If private apprenticeship programs are not available, many people believe that some sort of made work should be started which would take up the slack for idle teen-agers. Inventories of what needs to be done should be taken by local governments. Certainly our cities have vast areas which are blighted. These could be cleaned up, repaired, painted, planted and made appetizing again. Such an approach in some areas might be far cheaper and far more desirable than merely bulldozing the area, killing off the neighborhood personality, and putting up high-rise housing developments which often breed worse conditions than the ones they attempt to correct.

We all know that certain broken-down neighborhoods can be restored to dignity, even to fashion, when people care enough to do something about it. There's no reason why large segments of our teen-agers couldn't be put to work doing such jobs, learning while they worked. President Kennedy, in a broadcast early in 1961, said he hoped to use the Peace Corps concept in slum and depressed areas in this country, as well as abroad. Several other officials have said the same. There is no reason why this cannot be done, but it would not solve delinquency if only young men of the present Peace Corps age bracket were used. They are much older than those who form the core of the problem. Reviving the old Civilian Conservation Corps, also on the Kennedy agenda, would help, but work in the cities would be more educational and more meaningful, since CCC training, on the whole, leads to no career but merely postpones it.

In general, the important thing is to have a variety of work and training opportunities which will keep kids off the streets and busy at something *they* like and believe has a future.

2. *Schools.* The school problem, of course, is closely tied to the work problem, for so many of our delinquents are recruited from the nonlearners, the bored and the others who don't fit into our present curricula. The Secretary of Health, Education, and Welfare, Abraham Ribicoff, is among many interested persons who believe that our school laws should be revised to allow certain students to leave earlier. But if this is not feasible, it's quite possible to build work programs right into the schools. Youngsters who prefer to work with their hands rather than with books can then have jobs, get academic

credits and earn some money at the same time. There is no reason why our schools, compelled to accept all comers, should educate them as if they all had the same basic needs.

Beyond that, schools must do much more to see that the non-learner is at least taught to read and write with some proficiency even if it means dropping most other subjects to do so. It is astonishing what a close corollary often exists between illiteracy and delinquency. At New York's Youth House, a detention center for delinquents, it was found that 85 percent of the youngsters could not read at their grade level.

Much more could also be done with delinquency prevention in the schools. A schoolteacher sees more of a child than anyone else, except the parents. Potential trouble can, and should, be spotted earlier. It has been estimated that in 90 percent of the cases the delinquency pattern is already set by the age of eleven. If this is so, and detection is made at an early age, then the necessary factors and services could be brought to bear to straighten the child out. It is necessary, of course, to have such factors and services on hand. It does little good to detect a delinquent if nothing is done about it.

In the matter of detection, it is surprising that more schools haven't shown interest in the delinquency prediction scale invented by Drs. Sheldon and Eleanor Glueck, of Harvard. This device, which resulted from the Gluecks' ten-year study of five hundred delinquents matched with five hundred nondelinquents, showed that there are five factors influencing delinquency: father's discipline, mother's supervision, father's affection, mother's affection and the family's cohesiveness. Using these factors, which sharply differentiated the two sets of youngsters, the Gluecks have been able to predict delinquency in schoolchildren with astonishing accuracy.

They do not claim 100 percent infallibility. But their system is as reliable as the actuarial tables of insurance companies, which it strongly resembles. In Boston and New York, retrospective studies of delinquent boys have proven the Gluecks' prediction tables 90 *percent accurate*. Current Japanese and French studies show similar accuracy with the same tables, despite the fact that these countries' cultures are different from ours.

The Gluecks' system has been attacked in the profession on the ground that it is undemocratic, that it spots and determines a young-ster's career, and brands him as a delinquent even though he may never become one. The Gluecks, on the other hand, do not feel it brands a youngster any more than an I.Q. test does. They say it is simply another aid, a social Geiger counter, that can spot delin-quency *probability* and possible danger so that measures can be taken to correct the situation. They feel that the results of such testing can be kept secret from the child just as the results of I.Q. testing are kept secret. And they see no reason why a school principal, or a probation officer, or a judge should not know the statistical proba-bility of delinquency in the child he is dealing with any more than an insurance company should not know the statistical probability of a person's life expectancy when it is insuring him.

If we bear in mind that there is no infallibility in any testing of this kind, the Gluecks' scale could be one more aid in the battery of weapons which schools can offer to help spot juvenile delinquents before they get to the arrest, or court, stage.

3. *Probation.* Most thoughtful people in the field will agree that *if* probation is adequate, it can do more to straighten out the ma-jority of kids who land in juvenile court than any other approach. It is certainly cheaper than an institution—roughly one-tenth the cost. And yet almost nowhere are our probation services up to par, either because of a lack of trained personnel or because low wages soon force people out of the profession.

In addition to raising salaries, we might do what the English have done—start special, accelerated, one-year courses for older people (over thirty) who want to enter this field. England draws widely on people in all branches of life to fill such posts—retired army officers, schoolteachers, sportsmen, clergymen, business people, housewives and just warm human beings. "A good heart is more im-portant than a flock of degrees," a British official told me, and the recidivism figures there would indicate the English are on the right track.

To help further our overworked probation staffs, we might also do what just about every other country in the world has found worth-while—develop a corps of volunteers who can work with the pro-fessionals but whose case loads are limited to two or three youngsters.

We might also pay such people small stipends, so that good people of small means would be able to meet the necessary expenses of carfare, trips, etc.

4. *Police.* Although there are some excellent and dedicated juvenile police officers, most people who visit our country are, on the whole, unimpressed with the caliber of policemen who deal with children. In most cities, in fact, top-quality police are rarely assigned to children's duty; they are usually well-meaning but incompetent staffers whom the chief doesn't know what else to do with.

Furthermore, all too often the regular police are unnecessarily hostile and lacking in sympathy. In California not long ago, a seventeen-year-old boy who had never been in trouble before decided to rifle some telephone boxes. They happened to be fitted with alarms, and before he knew it, the boy found himself confronted with a policeman. When the latter started interrogating him, the youngster panicked and started to flee. The officer, who already had his gun out, shot and killed him on the spot—all for stealing some coins from a phone box.

Such a case is extreme, but it points up the fact that, generally speaking, our police are, as a young English social worker who'd spent a summer working in this country said, "Too tough, too quick on the trigger!"

One street worker, who has spent ten years working with gangs and has seen many of his boys worked over by the police with fists, belts and other weapons, feels that there should be some sort of psychological testing before police are issued weapons. "It's frightening to put the power of life and death in a cop's hands," he declared.

Although a policeman can be a symbol of law, order and help, too often he's looked upon by teen-agers as "The Man"—someone who's hostile, even sadistic, especially where members of another race are concerned.

5. *Courts.* In the last few years, a higher percentage of youngsters coming before our courts are being sentenced to institutions than ever before. We have seen, for example, how a New Jersey judge packed a couple of boys off to a reformatory just for painting the base of a statue. This is being done in the face of a truly appalling

rate of recidivism in this country which assures that the majority of kids so sentenced will eventually enter a life of crime. Judges should give greater thought to the consequences of a term in a lockup, and not use such institutions merely because, like Mount Everest, they are there, or because "a few months in a training school should do this kid some good." *In terms of rehabilitation,* it rarely does.

I. J. Shain, of the California Department of Corrections, who made a detailed study of our courts, found that juvenile court judges are far too moralistic and inclined to see things in the light of their own limited experiences. "Some believe that they can actually change the lives of boys and their parents with five minutes of advice from the bench," he said. One judge, for example, ordered a boy to mow the lawn regularly. When the father protested that he didn't have a lawn, the judge said, "I order you to put one in!" Another judge told a boy he could be straightened out by doing the family dishes every night (the judge had done the dishes every night when *he* was a boy). When the mother volunteered that the family had an electric dishwasher, the judge ordered her to turn it off.

One of the troubles with a large part of our courts, of course, is that the judge is not a specialist in juvenile cases, but merely doubles in that capacity when not handling adult ones. The reason for this is that the volume of juvenile cases in rural counties does not warrant a full-time judge of this kind. Most foreign countries, and three of our own states, however, have gotten around this condition by having a juvenile court judge serve for a number of counties. He moves from court to court as the volume of cases decrees, much like the old circuit rider.

6. *Institutions.* In general, our institutions defeat themselves by being far too large, by having children who shouldn't be there in the first place, and by keeping them too short a time for real rehabilitation. Furthermore, work as a therapy is not the guiding rule, and there is only the most halfhearted attempt to teach a child the satisfaction that comes from learning to do one thing well. Institutions are handicapped by our work-use laws, of course, but Chino's record in California has proven that when people want to do something about it, industry, labor and the general public are willing to cooperate.

Equally as important as the curriculum of our correctional institutions, however, is the basic need to develop alternatives to the institutions themselves—the halfway houses, the open homes, the attendance centers, the semi-liberty institutions, the apprentice homes, the probation hostels, the short-term arrest centers and all the other things in the bag of rehabilitative tricks which have been developed in the last few years so successfully in other countries where recidivism is far less than ours. But for some curious reason these things have been ignored here. In this country, the astonishing fact is that we have developed *no widely accepted alternative except a few forestry camps.* This gap must be filled.

7. *Experts.* In general, the American public has abdicated its rights to the scientists in dealing with delinquents. As Judge Kohler has said, "We leave everything to the specialists here. In Europe everyone gets in the act, and the results are far better."

Unfortunately, the trouble with experts and agencies in the field is that they tend to become empire builders. They are dedicated to proving that *their* methods work so that they can get more money and more prestige for what *they* are doing. They are not particularly interested in organizing the total community to fight the problem.

Furthermore, American specialists seem to have an almost mystical obsession with the idea of research, and many won't move in any direction until it's been "proven" that this is the right direction. However, research never seems to give us such proof (at least to the satisfaction of all), and so it just becomes an end in itself. Research, or as some critics call it, nose-counting, is often used in place of imagination and common sense. Overdone, it leads to absurd results. One expensive survey, for example, analyzed small children for "succorance and playmirth," which simply means the youngsters' seeking of fun and companionship. After many months had passed, many dollars been spent and many tabulations made, the tremendous scientific conclusion was revealed like a thunderclap from Mount Sinai: little boys like to play with little boys, and little girls with little girls!

One scientist, fed up with all this, is Russell Kirk, the research professor at Long Island University who feels we've had enough of pseudo science in the behavior field. "Imagination in the long run rules the world—not scientific research, and still less, scientistic sham," he wrote in the *New York Times*. "Modern society, in many ways sick, needs not the short-sighted manipulations of the research technician, but rather the artist's touch."

Dr. John Conrad, the California criminologist, is another scientist who agrees with him, and feels the public should evince a little more skepticism regarding experts. "The trouble with the experts in the United States," he says, "is that they view delinquency as primarily an intellectual problem, and they have no particular concern for the people involved. If, for example, a man here wants to be a probation officer and offers as credentials the fact that he likes people and wants to help them, he probably won't get the job. He's suspect." As an example of what happens abroad, Dr. Conrad told me of a British probation officer he'd come across who said that he believed that it was within his power to help each person in his case load "come closer to the image of God."

"Can you imagine an American probation officer saying a thing like that?" asked Dr. Conrad. "It's not considered scientific!"

8. *Coordination.* In general, there is little coordination between agencies in this country—from state to state, city to city, or even neighborhood to neighborhood. "In Brooklyn, a juvenile delinquent can get three or four more years for a crime than he will get in Manhattan," said Aaron Schmais, of New York's Youth Board, who recently made a study of the situation for a Congressional committee.

It is heartening what can happen when people cooperate. A few years ago, Baltimore, tired of having the delinquency programs of police, court, schools, church and other organizations working at cross purposes with one another, made a real attempt to coordinate all their activities in one place—the juvenile court building. There, most of the community's public and private resources have offices or representatives, and the court is the hub around which the city's whole child welfare program rotates. Such close cooperation tends to eliminate waste and duplication, and most organizations can communicate with each other just by walking down the hall. With everybody looking in on everybody else all the time, higher standards are stimulated. Baltimore not only has one of the best juvenile courts in the country, but perhaps the most effective probation system, with case loads limited to fifty or sixty per officer.

The statistical results are gratifying. Baltimore's rate of delinquency has not increased since World War II. And the actual number of delinquents today is less than it was five years ago, despite a steady increase in the city's population. We could use a lot more of Baltimore's type of coordination.

9. *Tolerance.* Not long ago, John Crosby, the critic, revealed in his syndicated column that he stole, or "borrowed," iceboats when he was a teen-ager so that he could sail them. Today, iceboats aren't readily available in most cities, and kids steal, or "borrow," cars. This is not to be condoned, of course, but neither is it a reason to act as though such things never happened in another generation, and to take measures which exacerbate, rather than alleviate, the problem.

Many people also look on gangs as a recent phenomenon. And yet from time immemorial boys have been retreating into a private tribal life of their own by withdrawing from the community. Huck Finn and Tom Sawyer, those classic American youths, were part of a juvenile gang world which stole boats and did other things that would surely be considered delinquent today.

"We are oversensitive to deviant behavior today," says I. J. Shain. "There is no one of us who wouldn't be subject to juvenile court adjudication because of something he has done in the last six months, if we were truthful about it."

The rest of the world seems more resigned to a bit of hell-raising on the part of their youngsters, and accepts it as a part of growing up. They do not constantly widen the definition of delinquency to include every aberration. In the words of M. Morelli, the French Deputy Minister of Justice, quoted earlier, "The European accepts the adolescent for the half-man, half-child that he is, a creature of romance, passion and impulse."

Another European, the head of an institution abroad, put it this way: "Delinquency is a little like masturbation. It used to be considered a sure way to sin and insanity. Now psychiatrists tell us that almost everyone indulges in some form of masturbation, and so we don't get quite so excited about it. That's the way it should be with juvenile delinquency."

10. *Mass Media.* Little has been said in this book on the effect of television, the movies, comic books and the press in general on delinquency. The reason is that, although much is claimed, little is known about the subject. However, it seems only natural that the widening streak of violence that runs through our entertainment media, for example, must reflect itself in the action of our teen-agers, who in the last analysis are trying to be like grownups.

Heman Stark, director of California's Youth Authority, told me he has occasionally interviewed boys who, after robbing someone and getting the money they want, have then senselessly hit the victim over the head with their gun. When asked why they did it, each one exclaimed, "But that's the way it's done on TV!"

Taking time off to monitor some local TV stations one day, Stark noticed that each station averaged between twenty-five and thirty assaults in which somebody got knocked cold by being hit on the head. "On TV," he said, "the victim generally gets up and walks away, but in real life they don't."

The Senate Juvenile Delinquency Subcommittee recently monitored national TV programs put on between 4 and 10 P.M., and found that in the last seven years the programs devoted to violence have increased from 22 to 34 percent. The subcommittee also noted that in the same number of years the instances of brutality increased about 300 percent in the 7 to 10 P.M. period.

With the widening of our communications horizons in a fantastic way, crime gets coverage which people never dreamed possible fifty years ago. And as everybody knows, the power of suggestion is strong. A dramatic mad bomber story triggers a whole string of bomber stories—or suicides, or kidnapings, or teen-age rumbles.

"Your newspapers are filled with headlines about juvenile delinquency," a Danish official said to me. "Naturally your children end by feeling they must live up to the headlines."

It is interesting that in the French press there is a tendency to soft-pedal news of delinquency. There has been a tacit agreement among the newspapers to do so. "Lurid stories sell papers, but they also encourage kids to go off the deep end," said a French newspaper-man. "It's better to play the delinquency stuff down, better for all of us in the long run."

The French, whose delinquency is under control, have taken an equally strong stand on violence in movies, comic books and other literature for young people. They practice a tight censorship. In the matter of TV, they have been even more drastic. Although the French are notoriously open-minded about sex and censorship in general, they won't allow violence on the air, even for adults. They admit many of our most popular shows would be popular over there, but they simply don't think a diet of violence would be good for people, especially when it's so hard to prevent children from seeing the programs.

On the other hand, when a measure to prohibit certain films from being shown to children in New York State was introduced not long ago, it was attacked as "thought control" and the beginning of a "dangerous censorship." And when our television industry was attacked for its increasing violence, executives were indignant. They tried to confuse the issue by saying violence was part of both Shake-speare and the Bible.

In view of these circumstances, one wonders if, indeed, people are willing to pay the price for the kind of controls necessary to curb delinquency—or if they just want some other group to pay the price. Other countries don't insist on absolute proof that something is bad for their children. They simply act on their instincts, which are often sounder than the "proof" that comes from, say, nose-counting.

11. *Parents.* We all know that children learn by imitating their parents. And not long ago, a grandmother was caught wheeling her groceries home in a supermarket cart and then sailing the cart merrily down a ravine so she wouldn't have to return it. A check of the ravine showed twenty-six more carts which this gray-haired hooli-gan had similarly disposed of. It is obvious that this senile delinquent did not have much to teach her children.

Obviously, parents *can* control the problem in most cases. If they are warm and understanding in handling their children, if they provide the right moral background, if they make available the proper education, job and social opportunities, the situation would be largely solved. But the fact is that large numbers of parents do *not* do these things. Furthermore, it is not always their fault. Often, like their children, they are victims of a new society—affluent and fast-changing. There has not been time to adjust.

Puerto Ricans, for example, arriving here for the first time, find their traditional world swept away. New standards have replaced the old. Mothers get the better jobs, and somehow the father image, so crucial in controlling delinquency, is swept away too. The situation is equally serious with Southern Negroes who have flooded our Northern cities since World War II. It is probably no accident that Negroes, whose society is largely a matriarchy, have a delinquency rate out of all proportion to their numbers.

Other countries, of course, have similar difficulties. With the problems created by progress and modern living, they too find it hard to provide adequate father images for their kids. But in their case, being more work-minded than we are, there is often a substitute father available in the person of a master apprentice or some other job-training instructor. In this country such things are improbable. A street worker with a gang is often the only chance many kids have for any kind of a father image.

12. *The Delinquency Label.* In the long run, the best cure for delinquency is age. If a child can slip quietly out of his teens without a record, without being hardened into a criminal, the battle is won. However, if somewhere along the line the label of delinquency is pinned on him, it's hard to get rid of it. Schools know it, classmates know it, the neighbors know it, and the youngster is set apart. He begins to live the role.

We have seen how in middle-class neighborhoods the delinquency label is much harder to obtain than in a lower-class one, even though the misbehavior is the same. This may not be egalitarian, but it certainly makes the job of growing into a normal, adult citizen a lot easier. And the community and the taxpayer benefit in the long run.

Abroad, as we have seen, the stigma of being a delinquent is bestowed *only* when a youngster commits a crime for which an adult could be found guilty. We could profit by a similar system here.

"It is this public naming of the delinquent, and the resulting conception of himself as delinquent, which is the heart of the prevention problem," says Joseph Lohman, Chicago's one-time sheriff. "Ways and means must be developed for handling the problem without dramatizing young people as evil, and without labeling and making them delinquent."

13. *Housing Developments.* With our present income restrictions on those who live in low-cost housing, all the able, ambitious, talented people are forced to move out as soon as their wages touch a certain figure. And by draining off all the people who could bring leadership, character and an element of success to the community, the ones left behind are largely the failures, the relief recipients and those without initiative. This kind of housing ends up with the cruelest kind of segregation—segregation by ability. Far more flexible restrictions are needed if housing developments are not going to be hotbeds of delinquency.

It might also be a good idea, as was mentioned earlier in this chapter, to give some thought to saving slum neighborhoods which have rehabilitation possibilities rather than ripping them up and starting from scratch. It is hard to create a community feeling in a new housing fortress—at least for years. And unless the neighborhood is hopeless, the wiser course might be to try to restore it. Old buildings, if properly looked after, have a built-in warmth and personality.

There are, of course, many other facets of delinquency control. Some countries have developed unique gimmicks that seem to work for them. In Athens, the police have found the weapon of ridicule works well. They parade a delinquent through the streets of the city wearing a placard saying, "I'm a damn-fool delinquent!" or some equally direct bit of self-denunciation. The Russians, on the other hand, have found photography useful. They take pictures of young Muscovites when they've had too much vodka and are making a spectacle of themselves. Later, when the youngster has sobered up, they show him what he looked like. If he doesn't behave, they threaten to publish the picture. The threat often accomplishes its purpose.

As mentioned before, of course, no one approach, or even several approaches, will do the job. Different people react differently, and human behavior is difficult to prescribe for. Each community must have more than one trick up its sleeve.

But even while we're mobilizing such tricks, it's important to keep the problem itself in its proper perspective. This is part of the therapy. Let us remember, for example, when we read an outraged editorial calling for war on our teen-agers, or when we read that a boy of fifteen has been sentenced to the electric chair (which has happened while this is being written), that given our way of life a certain amount of delinquency is inevitable. Given our rapid urban revolution which has brought a good part of our population from the rural sections to the cities, given our rapid mechanization, given our unparalleled prosperity, given our work laws and our insistence that everyone stay in school until sixteen or seventeen whether he's learning anything or not, given our general prolonging of youth and its economic dependency despite a natural longing to be independent, and given the inability of an able-bodied boy to get a job, there is bound to be a disruption, a behavior lag until things are shaken down and a more traditional and workable way of life eventually evolves. This, in essence, is the price of progress not only in the United States but in other countries the world over. "Stable societies are bothered little with volatile behavior," says Dr. Henry D. McKay, of the Chicago Project. "When the rate of change is high, as it is in the modern American city, then delinquency is highly destructive."

During this rate of change, it is important to remember, too, that things are not quite so bad as they seem with our youngsters. They are *not* turning the land into a lawless jungle, as some would have us believe. While in my home state last summer certain high school boys and girls were pulling off thrill robberies and stealing cars and making headlines that were selling papers, the vast majority were going about the business of trying to become adults in as orderly a fashion as always. In fact, three of them accomplished the rare achievement of hitting the front pages *without* committing a delinquent act. Joseph Geller, sixteen, Michael Bandrowski, sixteen, and Alfred Siefker, seventeen, spent their days hunting fossils in the Jersey Meadows like adult scientists, and were rewarded with a glittering prize that the most distinguished paleontologist would have been proud of. They turned up a fossilized gliding reptile, 175 million years old and previously unknown, that represents the first animal with a backbone ever to soar through the air. The American Museum of Natural History was so impressed it requested the animal, and ended up giving the boys a stipend.

Few kids become celebrities and reap status so fortuitously today, but the vast majority do want to grow up normally and do grown-up things. "Most kids turn out all right eventually," says Karl Holton, "but they've got to have help and understanding. Any kid who never gets into trouble isn't worth raising."

And when they do get into trouble—real trouble—it's important not to panic and do things which will get a lot of other kids in trouble too. Let's expect trouble, in fact, and be ready with whatever is needed at the moment—a psychiatrist, a job, a doctor, a drug, an electroencephalogram, a different educational program, a junior apprenticeship, a center like Highfields or, in the last extremity, a small training school or reformatory where the youngster will be taught some trade and be really rehabilitated. Only by bringing up a whole arsenal of ammunition, *and by being willing to accept a limited objective for each one,* can we slowly but surely get the delinquency figures going down rather than up. There is no easier way.

Some time ago, Prime Minister Macmillan of Great Britain was discussing in the United Nations the subject of peace, a subject which, according to public opinion polls, is the only one which concerns people more than juvenile delinquency. He ended his speech by giving a formula for achieving his objective.

"I am sure," he said, "that the less dramatic but the more practical way is this: the only way forward is by a *gradual* approach and working step by step in *practical* ways to improve the position. We need to work patiently and sincerely all the time. We need to remember that the hopes of millions of people are fixed upon us . . . and for their sakes, we must not fail."

This blueprint for peace among nations can be equally valid in achieving peace among our youth. For, in the last analysis, the two are closely related: the peace of tomorrow depends on the youth of today.

INDEX

Turkey
  and delinquency, 5, 56
  and the father, 88–89
  student riots in, 21, 54

Unemployment and youngsters, 135
Unions
  and apprenticeships, 132, 142, 143, 153
  and Chino, 155
  and delinquency, 134–135
  and gang work projects, 125, 179
United Nations London conference, 28, 55
Utah, 94, 171–172

Villages
  apprentice, 136–137
  children's, 174–175
Violence, 36
  of crimes, 20–23, 26–27, 30–31
  and entertainment, 193–194
Virginia
  Fairfax Child Clinic, 16
Volunteers as probation officers, 161–166

Washington, D.C., 57
Weapons, 65–66
Westchester County, 58, 59
White House Conference on Children and Youth, 1960, 12, 134
Whittick, R. J., 52
Work and boys, 77–78, 110, 156–157
  as deterrent to delinquency, 138–139
  meaningful, 118, 120–121, 138–139, 183–185
  as preventive, 183–185
  as therapy, 153, 155, 169, 189
Work-study programs, 124

Youth Arrest Home, 170–171
Youth Authority, California's, 149, 151
Youth Board, New York, 113, 114, 132
Youth Conservation Corps, 125–129, 134
  national, 140–141
Youth for Service, 178–180
Youth worker, *see* Street worker

Zack, Alvin, 134, 135

Set in Intertype Garamond
Format by Howard Burg
Manufactured by American Book—Stratford Press, Inc.
Published by Harper & Brothers, New York